Lucifer's Journey to Planet Earth

SHORT LOVE STORIES AND MESSAGES FROM LUCIFER

Nika Jones

 FriesenPress

Suite 300 - 990 Fort St
Victoria, BC, V8V 3K2
Canada

www.friesenpress.com

ISBN
978-1-4602-9972-2 (Hardcover)
978-1-4602-9973-9 (Paperback)
978-1-4602-9974-6 (eBook)

1. RELIGION, INSPIRATIONAL

Distributed to the trade by The Ingram Book Company

Table of Contents

I dedicate this book to my forever-lasting loves from planet Earth: *women.*

—*Lucifer*

Love is pure you, unused and unaltered.

Foreword

Who is Lucifer?

"Lucifer is the Latin name for the 'Morning Star,' both in prose and poetry, as in works by early Latin writers."[1] His name also translates from Latin as "Light Bringer." In the Christian religion, he is evil. He is also a symbol of disobedience. Different cultures and eras give different descriptions of Lucifer and his duties. This book focuses on the Light Bringer aspects of Lucifer's mythology by capturing moments from his love life.

Who is Nika Jones?

I am a Canadian citizen who was born in Romania. My interest and passion for writing started a long time ago, in my childhood. Due to the waves of life that were always pushing me in all directions, I could not pursue that passion until now.

---

1 Wikipedia contributors, "Lucifer," *Wikipedia, The Free Encyclopedia*, https://simple.wikipedia.org/w/index.php?title=Lucifer&oldid=5359714 (accessed October 18, 2016).

During my life, I changed my career many times in order to support my family. As an immigrant, I had to constantly start new jobs in different fields. I worked in the programming and computer field, later switched to insurance, and then to property management.

I am an intuitive healer, and during my life I have practiced yoga and learned astrology and numerology.

I've always been interested in the unseen parts of this universe. Even when I was young, I would ask my parents and teachers many questions about the invisible world. The fewer answers I received, the more my passion grew. My enthusiasm increased over the years, and it is exciting for me now as I answer my own questions through channellings (communicating with any consciousness that is not in human form—it is a form of esoteric communication) and direct writing.

Right now, we humans are in a very exhilarating place in our evolution, and I recommend that each one of you tries channelling. The magic of channelling is hard to explain, because it is an interpretation of "light language." This is an interdimensional language that translates into words what we all can understand at the soul level. The source, or other high frequency beings, send their divine codes or information to be translated into our language for our understanding, which is then processed through our intuition.

As per Wikipedia, "Intuition is the ability to acquire knowledge without proof, evidence, or conscious reasoning, or without understanding how the knowledge was acquired. Different writers give the word "intuition" a great variety of different meanings, ranging from direct access to unconscious knowledge, unconscious cognition, inner sensing, inner insight to unconscious pattern-recognition and the ability to understand something instinctively, without the need for conscious reasoning."

Your body does that automatically when you tune into the right frequency. We are like a radio. When the radio is set to the right frequency, we listen to music or the news, and when it is not, we just hear noise, or nothing. For me, it is easy to put myself on the right frequency by using music or meditation. Most of us don't accept channelling as real, but when you try it, you will feel the magic, and you will want to do it forever. There is no need for special skills, because we have these skills dormant in us. Just trust the process and let it happen.

I had never read any books about Lucifer, and I was not interested in his life. I definitely believed what my religion told me about Lucifer, but now I am discovering another part of him, and that is very fascinating to me. I could never imagine him being in love, or loving women with the intensity that he explains through his love stories.

With this in mind, last year I had a big surprise when Lucifer reached me. I needed time to think if I would communicate with him or not. Shortly after that, I contacted him, because I felt a strong curiosity to find out what he was doing. I knew he had returned to the source thirty years ago, but I hoped to hear further news on the progress of his ascension. Therefore, I channelled him. Instead of answering my questions about ascension, he opened our conversation with love stories and love poems. Being puzzled, I asked many questions, and since then I have enjoyed our lovely conversations. I noticed a powerful love energy entering my field while we talked.

Besides love stories, Lucifer has also given us a few messages about life in general, which can help us to understand why things are the way they are. I struggled my entire life as I searched for the answers to the "big whys" of my life. *Why that happened to me? Why me?* It always irritated me that I didn't know *why*.

Therefore, I had to fight with myself to enhance my understanding and open my mind to receive Lucifer's messages. This inspired me to accept the big picture of life much better and to understand the answers to those big whys.

This magic started for me years ago, when I began channelling a few entities, among them are God, Jesus, Anunnaki, and my twin flame (the other part of your soul is called your twin soul or twin flame). I was interested in learning more about their existences in their dimensions and in receiving messages that can help our understanding and open our mind toward wisdom. We have lived for too long in ignorance and insensitivity, and I guess it is time for something new, and for new knowledge.

When I commenced this book, I didn't know that Anunnaki was the same entity as Lucifer. After doing some research, I found out that they are both the leaders and rulers of the underworld. From a cultural and historical point of view, he and his guys are Sumerian gods. With this in mind, I asked Lucifer for clarification. He told me that Anunnaki is the same entity as Lucifer, but that "Satan" and "the Devil" are not his names, but rather his job titles used by different cultures in distant eras.

I asked Lucifer, "What is the name of your planet in this universe?"

He replied, "Terra Five." He explained that Terra Five is a parallel Earth, with a vibration that is higher than our Earth. He specified that his planet is not visible to us.

"We know about Nibiru being your planet," I said.

He replied, "Nibiru was occupied by the greys, and at this time, they have moved to another planet at the edge of our universe."

I then asked him how he travels between planets. He told me he moves via the materialization and dematerialization of his body and that sometimes he uses small transportation vehicles that you call unidentified flying objects on your planet. However, most of the time he travels using dematerialization, as it is almost instant.

It came as surprise to me when he said that he is the "Alpha and Omega."

"That is God," I said.

He replied, "That is true; God is Alpha and Omega of all universes—and all that is, and all that is not—but I am the Alpha and Omega of Earth. I am the bringer of both darkness and light on your planet. I am the beginning and the end—or the new beginnings, I can say. If your planet didn't graduate toward evolution (ascension in the end of year 2012) and began anew, you would be at the end of your existence right now."

Until that moment, I had only known about his dark side, and now he was telling us about his light, love, and angelic side. I always knew Lucifer as the bad guy—the one who would keep us in hell if we were not as good as religion teaches us to be. It was a surprise for me to see the light-and-love side of Lucifer.

In the beginning, I felt that I could not write this book, because it is very unusual. But considering the way this book helped me, I thought it might help you discover why events in your life happened the way they did.

But, I am grateful to have the opportunity to share these stories with you. In addition, Lucifer promised to give me love stories about more women for another book. How interesting would that be? He has his own style when he tells stories, sending them to me with his love energy. I felt that.

Lucifer mentioned that he would prefer it if the energy of the book remained vivid and profound. The love stories—and his messages—are powerful and short. I left them the way I perceived them. This whole book was channelled from July 2015 to summer of 2016.

The character's names and the places used in this book are changed from original message, as per Lucifer's desire. The love stories are taken from different eras over the past half-million years. He said the love stories are real, and they are told exactly the way they happened.

I hope you enjoy his writing style, because I left it the way I received it.

—*Nika Jones*

Introduction

Hello, fellow humans. My name is Archangel Anunnaki, and I am well known as Lucifer on planet Earth. Later on, you advanced my name from Lucifer to many other names, such as Satan, the Devil, Beelzebub, Belial, and more, all according to your culture and era. Therefore, you surrounded my name with the low energies of fear, panic, disgust, and horror. Every time someone mentions my name, your nervous system boosts the adrenaline hormone in your body. This produces a serious fear, and so you try to run away or close the conversation because you are not comfortable when speaking of me. Yes, I am Lucifer, and now I will tell you about my love adventures with the most delightful and attractive women on your planet.

Furthermore, I do not deliver this to clear my name from the energy that surrounds it. That would be nice, but this is not my intention. I deliver this to give you a complete understanding about our journey on planet Earth, because I am the one responsible for dropping your vibrations for a short time through fear.

In case you don't know, I have been in and out of your world for over one million of your years, and I loved humans, and I valued them. I created many jobs for your forefathers, who worked as miners for me, giving up on their low-paying fishing jobs.

When I designed this work, I selected just individuals who

needed more than they had. So, I guaranteed them plenty of money if they helped me to take the gold out from the mountains. I brought technologies from my world to yours to complete the job much more quickly and smoothly. Most of you honoured me and my guys, and you considered us your gods. We had a nice time together, and we lived in harmony and love for a long time. In that time, you lived without fear, and you surrounded me with respect and appreciation.

Before I showed up to Earth, you were angels who played in the Garden of Eden, as per your manuscripts. In that time, you were in harmony with the source/God/creator and the planet's electromagnetic force. In the meantime, you were peaceful and lovely fellas.

After a while, you aspired to separate yourselves from the source. You hoped to play by yourselves for a limited time in a lower dimension that was full with many contradictions and conditions. You just kept free will, which was your ticket to fly back to where you came from if you preferred to go out of the matrix. The matrix—or light grid—is an energetic web that surround the planet. In order to free yourself from the matrix, you have to raise your physical bodily vibration by raising your consciousness level through acts of kindness, unconditional love, and compassion.

Your free will played a significant role in your creation. Your free will is also responsible for the world you are creating that is manifesting itself through the thoughts, choices, and decisions you make. I have chosen to be the one who will serve to carry out your wish. Thus, we prepared a contract with an expiry date. When the day comes, I am supposed to go back to the light to restore my body to my pure form as archangel. The same applies to you. You are in the course of renewing your body and raising your vibration to reach a peace-and-love state of being.

When I started this project, I had to lower my frequency as much as possible so that I could be visible to your world. I had to erase my nervous system, but I held onto just one sentiment: the love and passion I have for women.

Why is that, you ask? Well, I can explain it to you now. I needed my bloodline to spread over your world so I could use it to reach you. I chose the most remarkable human women to be my brides. I love luxury, glamour, romance, grace, style, and refinement. Can you blame me for that?

There is just one thing I have to clarify: I never had your women if they were married or engaged. I had only available women—those with no strings attached. You see, while I kept my love for women, I always respected men, and I didn't want men to be hurt in their love lives. I had the whole planet at my knees, but I didn't want what belonged to you.

Even now, many souls on your planet think that my physical looks are those of a beast, with a tail, horns, and a demonic expression. This is far from the truth. Do you think that with those looks I could wed any woman on your planet? I don't think so. Seeing my pictures as portrayed by humans, I realize why so much fear is transmitted between you when speaking of me. You made me resemble a goat. Why are you frightened by goats? I don't understand. Now, my dear partners in duality, I can say that I would not get anybody close to me if I looked like that. Of course, I can improve or alter my body easily, because I am the fallen angel from the Bible. The absolute truth is that I am not a fallen angel—I am a descended angel. My looks are like yours, and we are both a part of the same source.

On the other hand, we had a contract. Do you remember that? Both parties signed it. It is as in theatre, where the actors sign a contract to perform a role. We did the same. I played my character, and the humans played theirs. We agreed and signed on to our journey on planet Earth.

While we worked together on this project, we were highly enthusiastic, and we demanded to start it right away. The source/creator knew that we might run into the possibility that we couldn't restore ourselves to our earlier condition without the source's aid. That's why the source mother/father proposed to participate in this game for a limited time. After that, I would have to come back to my earlier archangel form, and you to your previous forms as angels of light. We would only receive help from the source if we couldn't do it by ourselves.

Guess what? We couldn't do it by ourselves. We destroyed ourselves a few times. Do you remember that? If you do not remember, please check out your history textbooks.

Around thirty years ago, God called me home because of the suffering I had created for humanity. It was time to go back to the light. Now I am pure light, and my body is restored to my earlier condition. I am working with archangels, ascended masters, and other light beings to bring back your bodies to your earlier statuses as angels of light.

Thank you, dear ones, for the great pleasure I had with you, and for the experiences we produced together in this journey. Those experiences are like diamonds on your planet, precious and adored by heaven.

Thus, I returned to my form as archangel, and now I am working with many helpers to reinstate you as angels of light. This means you are going back home as light beings. You are no longer in my custody, and you will play in the new Garden of Eden for however long you choose.

In this garden, you will discover unconditional love under the *law of one*. I specified this because you will enter into another contract when it becomes available again. This is optional, as no one is pushing you to enter any contracts. In God's garden, there will be no free choices, nor any free will. You affect the wellbeing of your society's members when you are not in balance and harmonization with the source—and with yourself.

Your bodies will be readjusted to take in the light from heaven. This project started years ago. Now we are in the last phases of working towards lifting you up to your abilities. This means you will receive aid to activate each one of your bodies.

With great love, from your partner in business,

—Lucifer

1

Your Journey Home

I know how hard is for families to lose their loved ones. I lost mine many times because they were mortal, and I wasn't. It's an immense pain, but I got all of you back in my life after you passed on to the other side of the veil. I had to do that because you belonged to me, according to the contract. So, I developed a place for you where you could continue your life without an earthly body. The place I created is called heaven. I put you to work to give you the illusion that you could carry out here the richness you experienced on Earth. I didn't pay you for your job, but I made you work for at least eight hours a day. For the souls who wished more for their families, I built a bonus program, and according to the number of achieved bonuses, I gave them free houses—not to own, but for them to care for.

I also created places to help the damaged souls regenerate. You worked efficiently to help other souls, and I created many work departments according to your skills and experiences. After you left your body, you ended up in dark places that you call hell. I left you there for a while to burn up all of your desires and fears. After that, I sent the salvage team after you to pull you up from your own hell. Most of you lived in this mind-created hell for hundreds of earthly years, until we pulled you up into so-called heaven. I gave you the impression that beyond this heaven, there were many steps to take in order to grow higher into the light. I had to do that because beings from your Earth families, which lived in higher dimensions, were visiting you often.

Here, you waited for your loved ones to come from Earth so you could live together. After a while, you go back to the reincarnation department to arrange your trip back to Earth. You had to resolve the issues you hadn't solved while reincarnated on Earth. You chose your family members, friends, country, and all the details that your soul needed to have as experience.

It's a wonderful process, but I made it look ugly for you; I made you afraid of crossing over to another dimension. That was indispensable for your evolution. You need to have fears, otherwise you become immortal or you live too long. I didn't need you to become immortal—that was messing up with my plans. The longer you lived, the more dangerous it was for me to keep you under my spell of so-called amnesia. The strategy was to make you live for just a short time. Living longer means you have enough time to learn and become wiser. Living longer and becoming wiser wasn't on my agenda. I didn't want you to find out who you were, because that would make your experiences in third dimension impossible. It was easy to shorten your life; I just had to create many things that would send your nervous system into adrenaline mode. Thus, I am guilty for the fear you have, as I created the conditions for fear to take effect.

You accumulated many adventures on planet Earth, and many of you experienced serving as beings who were cut off from the source—and from each other. You agreed to reduce your frequency levels as much as you could; that was the contract. You achieved that with flying colors, and now I release you from my care and return you to God's hands.

I will tell you now, what happened to you after you died.

First, you should understand that I used your belief system, and I implemented features you were never aware of. I implemented different beliefs in different cultures, so that you might disagree with each other about who is correct and who is incorrect.

Once my work with your belief system was done, I altered your nervous system by implementing fear through various sources. Once fear was installed, your life was shortened.

Hundreds of years ago, I had to concentrate on your families. I had to start that because the women didn't work, and they married men who were supposed to support them. The woman's job was to have a family and take care of husband and kids. So, I destroyed that. Why, you ask? I had to make you unhappy, and your husband too. So, little by little, I had to pay your husband less and less to make you get a job, and I had to create jobs for you.

Also, I had to deliver the belief that you are inferior to your male counterpart, then I paid you less, and the gender difference was created. Why did I do that? When you had to go to work, your families were broken, and you had no time for a love life, no time to spend with your child, and no time to take care of your husband. I had to pay you less and less so I could get you to work more and more hours to make sure you had no time for your personal life. With this came stress, illnesses, disorders, sadness, depression, and anxiety. Those were the weapons I used to shorten your life. I was very successful, wasn't I?

Before you died, I mixed up your nervous system by introducing you to the fear of death. When your body lives in fear, your body vibration/frequency is very low. Therefore, after you left Earth, you ended up in my energetic containers that had been prepared for you, and they were called hell. You know there is no hell, and so when you prayed to God, we captured your requests and we dragged you up into so-called heaven. We moved you into another place, where your existence became finally better, and you believed that was paradise.

But your exploitation didn't cease there; it continued until now, when my energetic containers are destroyed, and the souls I had are free. Your deceased friends and relatives are now with God. My guys have just a few individuals working for them now, who were all kept captive. These souls swore to us under the oath that they would serve us. In exchange, we had to make them rich while living on Earth. These souls belonged to the dark beings. They still exist, but I am not their leader anymore. They have another leader now, and their living quarters are out of your galaxy. God arranged for them to exist in a place far away from you.

Most of my guys returned to the light, but not all of them. The ones who didn't return to light don't understand it, and they fear truth and love. They do not cherish or love each other, and they do not have programs to recover their own species. Usually, they leave behind their sick or hurt, abandoning them to die. Yes, they die too, but they live thousands of years if they are lucky, and they do not lose their body in wars, disasters, or accidents. They have many advanced technologies to heal, and move around the space, and they are cute, sharp, and smart.

Therefore, most of my guys do not believe in light, and they do not want to follow God's laws. They are part of God's creation, and they have their part to play in this universe, as well as other universes. As per my knowledge, they will continue to exist as long as the source wants them to exist. They are under the surveillance of light beings, and the light beings are monitoring all of their moves. Therefore, they are carefully watched—but they don't know that.

I know this will appear as a surprise to you, but this is what we achieved together. Both parties got out of this contract very successfully. I am extremely delighted by your achievements, and I congratulate you from the bottom of my heart for your strength and virtue in being a part of this experiment. Experiences that we have created together are divine, sacred, and priceless. No souls in this universe have ever achieved what we have accomplished together.

It was not a comfortable task for you or for me. This was very hard for both parties but I am glad it is completed and that you can return to light. You are God's angels, and he wants you to qualify for this trip back home. He will send all of his angels and light beings to help you on your path toward illumination and union with the source.

You are in the last phases of your journey towards liberation from the dark beings. You won the ticket to return to your original paradise. I am now your servant working with a big army of light to bring you on the perfect path toward home.

We are overjoyed to celebrate your arrival home after such a long journey. Remember, you are dearly, unconditionally loved.

With blessings, love and light, from your partner in business,

—*Lucifer*

2

Loving You as Loving Me

When you love yourself, you understand that you need to extend your love to somebody else. The feeling of being loved back is so powerful, and it is the most appealing feeling that our bodies can have.

I already introduced myself to you. My nickname is Aki in this form, and I am a perfect-looking male; I am tall with a regular weight, fine dark hair, and big, blue eyes. I can inform you that I look like a male model from planet Earth. Many women fell in love with my physical appearance. The love energy carried inside my heart was a male energy, one filled with passion, sensuality, and romance, as I searched for the love of my life. And as you know, my lifespan is endless, and so is yours, so I can say you are eternal, too. The fact that in the third dimension you have to keep changing your bodies makes you only temporarily mortal.

I was a fickle guy, because I cheated on all my women. Under my circumstances of immortality—you must understand—I couldn't stay just with one woman for eons of time. On each timeline, I had at least ten women, the most gorgeous of them. I had to do that because I had to get my bloodline going fresh on planet Earth. At the same time, I was bored on your planet, and I had to supply my life with interesting women.

Because I had so many women, I had to create an escape plan. My lovely women from planet Earth knew that I was not a husband who would stay home and help around the house. Each one of them knew that I was a businessman, and that I had to live away from home—sometimes for months at a time—in the mountains to work. I was outside of planet Earth, and so I needed a reason for not being home. My women agreed with my conditions, and they still wanted to be my wedded wives. I had to do that because my love and respect for women made me disclose my program to them. I wouldn't trick any of them to be with me in such situations if they didn't accept my conditions.

Now I will tell you a few love stories I had on planet Earth with Ada, a special entity who is my best friend in eternity.

One day, on the other side of the veil, Ada was arranging her human body. She had to live in a lower dimension for a limited time. Ada wanted to explore unconditional love in a dimension that was full of conditional emotions. This was an unlikely goal to achieve while still on planet Earth, but she wanted to try it. In other words, Ada realized that the energy on Earth would not permit such genuine love experiences.

While she prepared for her first incarnation, I said, "Darling, I will be glad to help you to achieve what you choose while living on planet Earth. I will be around helping humanity with their projects, and it would be a pleasure for me to help you too."

Ada agreed, replying, "It is such a great pleasure to have my best friend helping me with my project. I predict that you will fill my life with magic and fun, just as you are doing now. With your magnetism, this journey is going to be fantastic. However, you will be aware of my project, but I will not. How are you going to hide everything from me?"

"I will figure out a way to keep your project silent and hidden from you. If you succeed, I would love to be the one who makes it happen for you."

"Oh, my dear! I would love for that to happen, and I assume you will do an excellent job helping me to complete my experiment."

So, I did it. I kept my promise.

Around five hundred thousand years ago, Ada took a human body for the first time. Ada's devotion to undertaking something that potentially could not be achieved fascinated me. I realized that unconditional love was a difficult task to achieve on planet Earth, and was one with limited chances of success. But Ada was determined to try, and she was taking her chances with an unfavourable energy on such a magnificent planet.

However, while living on Earth, she would not be conscious of her project, her arrangements with me, or her other soul mates. Ada's memory had to be wiped out, and she wouldn't remember most of the contract. In the meantime, Ada would remain separated from the source, and she wouldn't recall our existence on the other side of the veil. Ada would occasionally perceive something, or recognize the people in her life from somewhere else, and she would listen attentively to her inner voice. But truly, she wouldn't recall much of this plan.

My dearest friend from eternity was unusually delighted by this idea. With this in mind, Ada moved to a lower-dimension realm, where she arranged her body shape and size, her parents, and her environment. Now my friend is happy and ready for her first journey in the third dimension.

Do you believe that Ada will achieve her project? What is love like on your planet? You should know by now.

I haven't forgotten it yet; it is disappointing, painful, hard, controlling, damaging, and depressing, but every life starts with a passionate fire called "falling in love." This love feeling brings you happiness, enjoyment, and pleasure, and it makes you lose your mind. Do you remember when you fell in love with your partner? This passion is what I am talking about, my dear. It doesn't matter if you perceive it or not. Every one of us, including me, spend our lives looking, seeking, and searching for the love of our life. So, nothing is surprising here.

When I showed up on planet Earth to find gold eons ago, and I met you, Ada, for the first time in a human body, I thought you were the gold I was searching for. I showed up in many of your lifetimes, just to be with you again. But you recognized me many times, and then choose something else. You often told me that you didn't perceive me as human, but you loved me for what I was, not for what I did to humanity. Many projects I didn't complete on many lifetimes because of your interventions, and you were not even conscious of that. My love for you was bigger than ruining your planet. I knew that you were a divine angel like I am, and that we were best friends on the other side of the veil. You didn't remember who you were, and this made you more extraordinary to me. It is simple to *be* when you know who you are. It is complicated to be when you have no indication of who you are. If I had to do what you are doing (taking a human body), I do not think I could handle it. But you are majestic and glorious and you dealt with the job perfectly. Congratulations!

In the meantime, I was your shadow for eons of time, and you spent your dreams with me many times. While I didn't need to hold any human emotions, I kept just one: the love and passion for the feminine goddesses.

Now I hope you realize, Ada, that the bloodlines on this planet are still developing from an ancient *you*, as well as other ancient women.

᧖

Now I will describe a few lives I spent with the love of my life from eternity, Ada. I will leave for another book my love adventures with other women. Indeed, I had a wonderful journey on your planet. In my own way, I loved each of the wives I had during my long trip on your planet.

While you read my love stories, you will notice more things about my personality, such as how I am good hearted, pleasant, charming, good looking, romantic, nostalgic, gentle, and loved. I do not want you to think that I am a perfect man, because I have my flaws. I am in love with Ada, and when she used a human body, I had to use many tricks to marry her, to have her with me all the time, or to have her attention. I have been with her during all of her reincarnations. When she took a man's body, I managed to become best friends with her, and so we were still close to each other. On other past lives, I was jealous of her twin flame, or soul mates. As you can see, being in love made me imperfect in my actions; however, my love for her—and for all my other women— was always pure and innocent.

These short love stories are like gold and diamonds to me, and you should know that your big treasure is called *love*. Human essence is love. Money, wealth, fame, glory, and so on won't bring anything good after you move to the other side of the veil. You cannot take those with you, but you will take the love from your heart into eternity. That love will shine everywhere in this universe.

With love,

—Lucifer

3

Falling in Love with You

It was a wonderful, sunny spring day, and it was time to find Ada, who was on a journey on planet Earth. We had both experienced unconditional love on the other side of the veil, and now we would experience the same love on planet Earth.

Her name was Diane in this lifetime, and I knew that she would be around eighteen years old by now. I made preparations to contact Diane, and I asked my business partners to help me find her.

We discovered her in a small city that is now modern-day Cairo. Diane was one of the loveliest creatures that God had created, and men were falling in love with her on the first date. My business partners arranged an invitation to a dance hall that Diane would be attending later that week.

I looked forward to dancing and talking with Diane, stealing her heart, and then getting married as fast as we could. Now was the time to start the unconditional love project with Diane on planet Earth. I was anxious to see if Diane would able to achieve her project, and I would be busy searching for the love that joined us in every lifetime.

Time went fast, and the day arrived. One of my business partners introduced me to Diane, and to other people. Watching her with excitement, enthusiasm, and passion, I fell in love right away.

Diane looked better than my glass technology had shown me. This is an advanced technology on my planet, and we use it to read, see, and watch Earth's past, future, and present, checking in on and examining people's lives. The best way to explain this technology is that it opens Diane's life book. Diane's lives—as well as yours—are recorded. The machine works by reading the Akashic records. You can compare the Akashic records for a better understanding with a library packed with documents. And I dared to look at Diane's record.

Even though I was the wealthiest guy on the planet, I was intimidated and excited by Diane's elegance, grace, refinement, and charm. After a while, I managed to recover from my temporary shock, and I asked her to dance with me. Diane quickly accepted the invitation, without reflecting much. She asked me to wait, because she had promised other men that she would dance with them that evening, and she could not refuse them now.

Looking fixedly in my eyes, Diane smiled and added, "Sorry, but the fifth dance will be yours, so please wait." I could read the demand in her big eyes.

Understanding the message, I replied, "It's a pleasure for me to wait, because I have the time on my side."

I had to stick around until it was my turn to dance with her. During this time, I observed Diane dancing and laughing. Time passed quickly, and then it was my time to dance. After our dance ended, I kissed Diane's hand, and I begged her to place me on her list for another dance that evening.

Diane laughed and said, "The next dance is yours. Happy? I canceled the other arrangements, assuming you will dance only with me the entire evening, if you do not mind. I acknowledge you are not from my city, so I decided to give you this chance to dance only with me."

How about that? Trying to stay calm, I said, "It would be an honour, darling, to keep you entirely to myself this evening."

I didn't know her intention, but this plan was brilliant. I noticed that my sweet friend preferred to dance only with me. While dancing with her, my heart was beating quickly, almost as if it was trying to leave the chest. We had a few dances together, and suddenly Diane asked me to go with her into the garden for a fresh air, if I didn't mind.

Are you kidding me? I thought. My excitement grew bigger upon hearing this great idea, and so I replied, "Yes, dear, I have a desire for fresh air, too."

We went out in the garden. Once there, Diane asked many questions about my family, profession, marriage situation, as well as other related questions.

Can you believe that I captured her interest so soon? When women ask questions, something is going on in their hearts. My heart pumped so fast, even though I was aware of who she was, and of our contract. However, Diane had no clue of our arrangement. I struggled to remain calm and serious, even though I wanted her to spend the rest of her life with me.

I arranged for another date for next day. Diane quickly accepted and said, "Something in you is so familiar, but I can't specify what it is."

Does she remember something from elsewhere? I wondered. Then I said, "My feelings are sending the same vibes, but I don't recall if we ever met."

After our conversation in the garden, I escorted her home. I politely kissed her hand, and then I said goodbye and began waiting impatiently for tomorrow. I had certainly provoked her curiosity, and she was interested in spending more time together.

The next day we met for an afternoon tea at a nearby teahouse. Diane looked like a shiny star in the night sky, but I had to play it cool and ask her questions. I expected to discover new things relevant to Diane's personality, and to encourage her fall in love with me. I had to use my entire selection of strategies to achieve that. We talked for a few hours about friends, family, art, music, and other subjects.

Before leaving, I proposed another date. I was living in my friend's house, so I took my chances and invited her for supper that evening. Diane agreed, smiling with satisfaction and delight. I perceived a vibe of enjoyment in my heart as I felt her powerful attraction for me. Every wave of love I received from Diane I kept in my heart for now.

Following this, we met each day—and sometimes a few times per day—until she fell in love with me. *Oh, my God! Diane will be my wife*, I thought. It was such an excellent feeling, and it made me dance and cry with happiness in my room. It wasn't easy with so many guys trying to grab her grace and heart. What made her choose me over other rivals? I never understood why, and I was not concerned to find out, but I loved her precious choice. I certainly met the criteria of a perfect lover and husband. So, hooray! Everything was working better than I had planned.

One day, she said, "Oh, dear, my perception is that I have seen you somewhere, and that is strange, because I never met a man as unusual as you."

I replied, "Well, I sense something too, but I do not think we have ever met."

After dating Diane for a few months, I proposed to her to marry me. One night, we went to an elegant restaurant, and there I surprised her with an impressive ring. Diane said that she agreed to marry me, because she thought that I would make a great husband and father for her future kids. We arranged to visit Diane's parents and to ask for their blessings. Diane loved her parents very much, and she didn't want to do something improper to upset them.

She said, "My parents are reasonable and proud people who love me from the bottom of their hearts, and I do not want to betray their trust."

I would talk to her father and pray to God that they would approve and accept me as their son-in-law. Diane arranged a supper for us at her house the following day so that I could meet and talk with her parents.

The next day, I showed up in the evening at her place, and Diane's father invited me inside. We had a drink together, and after a while, he began asking questions.

"Aki, why do you want to marry Diane? What are your qualities? Are you a better man than the others? Many of them have asked for Diane's hand in marriage. Diane hasn't decided yet which one she will choose. I have blessed them all, and Diane is still analyzing and thinking."

I said, "Well, Adam, I don't know what qualities other men have, but I have loved Diane from the day I met her. Since Diane stole my heart, I fell in love, and I cannot live without her. When she is not around, my heart and stomach hurt, and I cannot sleep. My love for Diane is increasing daily, and I will always love your beautiful daughter. Dear Adam, my wish is not to separate you from your daughter. Diane told me how much you love her, and how painful it will be for you when she marries. Without her in your life, you will be sad and unhappy. I live in another city, and I do not wish to take Diane away from your life. So, I will buy land, and I will build a house near your house. You are welcome to visit whenever you want, or to move in with us. Your wish will be a law for me."

Adam smiled with pleasure and gave me Diane's hand in marriage. He looked happy and content. I believe Adam noticed that I was a wealthy man, and that I could take a great care of her. In addition, I was comfortable around Adam, and we enjoyed our conversation. Diane's parents were nice people; they were friendly, gentle, modest, and appeared well educated.

Soon, the door opened, and Diane entered the room, inviting us for supper. Finishing the conversation and looking fixedly at Diane, I said, "Darling, Adam gave us his blessings. He is sorry because your mother is not with us to celebrate together on this big day."

Diane slowly approached her father, and then embraced and kissed him with love.

Anyway, we had a delicious dinner together while we arranged the wedding date and details. I suggested to Adam that he let me pay for wedding expenses. Adam agreed with the marriage arrangements, and he was ready to help if I needed any moral support.

I needed a few weeks to prepare the wedding as per Diane's wishes. We got married and had a sumptuous celebration. After the wedding, we left for our honeymoon, and when we came back, we lived with Adam until our house was ready. That was her father's demand, to keep us around him.

Time passed quickly, and Diane gave me four naughty kids.

Diane had no clue of my origins. She thought that I might be human, but even my image was better than any human on your planet. I provided everything for my family that their hearts dreamed of, wanted, and desired. I loved Diane with passion, but, along the way, she noticed my inhuman parts, and she questioned me again.

I remember one night when she saw that my eyes were different than normal. Diane described a gleaming light that she saw in my eyes, and she compared my eyes to a tiger's eyes.

I laughed, and I said, "My dear, your eyes are the same. It may be from the moonlight's rays."

To make the story short, our children's lives differed from those of other kids; ours had somewhat wild instincts. Diane questioned me again. Even if she was as an observer in our life, I loved her intensely, and I admired her for her entire life. Many times, when she detected something, she passed rapidly over everything that had disturbed her.

In that life, Diane lived ninety-two years, and every time she was sick, I healed her while she slept, and the next day she was perfect. When she was fifty years old, she became upset because I was looking younger than her (as an immortal thirty-year-old), and she suspected something.

She questioned me again. "Who are you? Why you don't age?"

I answered her, saying, "I am God!"

Then, she asked me to move out of the house. Oops! I had made a big mistake. This was my first life with her in the third dimension, and I had forgotten to change my age.

Because she asked too many questions, with regret I had to leave, but I checked in on her regularly. I was sad to take off, but she didn't give me any choice.

Our kids grew up and developed paranormal senses. Because Diane was truthful to God, she directed the kids how to use their God-given gifts to heal other people. Therefore, the kids were given a human mission, rather than their daddy's mission.

I had many women and many kids in that timeline. My wives were of different ages, and they resided in various countries. So, I married each one of them. None of my wives were conscious that I had cheated on them with other women. I know this is not nice, but I didn't have any other options at that time.

The love I had experienced and shared with Diane I never had with any other woman. Since then, she has held the key to my heart and all of my angelic love in the third dimension. We met further in other lifetimes, and we fell in love repeatedly, but she always suspected me of not being human. Other times, Diane told me why she loved me. She considered me an angel from heaven, and I liked that. I guess she thought of me as a talented provider. Every time we met in different lifetimes, she recognized me.

Our love fascinated and captivated me in a way I cannot describe. Diane's charm, sensuality, passion for love, and cleverness interested me the most. Our life was full of huge passions, with the fire of desire burning in our hearts, but she couldn't carry out her unconditional love in this particular life.

—*Lucifer*

4

Looking for My Love

When a sunny day arrived in early April, I thought it could be an excellent time to search for my lovely Ada.

Looking in my agenda, I saw that she would be approaching adulthood. Her name in this life was Rani. I prepared myself in order to impress my lovely friend. I made myself tall with blue eyes and light brown hair. I was a good-looking male who wanted to take his chances on another love experiment with his celestial love.

Before I could pay her a visit, I had to figure out where exactly she was on the planet. After a while, I spotted her in India, living a comfortable life with her parents. Rani was around sixteen years old.

At that time, teachers were visiting Rani's house. She had a great interest in learning how to paint the landscape, and so Rani's parents were looking for a teacher. I supposed this would be a great occasion to meet my lovely friend, and I hoped she would welcome *me* as her teacher. I guessed it was a perfect strategy to pop up in Rani's life again. It meant we would have to spend a lot of time outdoors in nature, making paintings and having fun. I downloaded the talents and knowledge of a teacher, and then I showed up to her house.

Her parents interviewed me for a while, and they seemed very interested in having me as Rani's teacher. And, in the end, they introduced me to Rani. I presume that I touched them with my skills as a designer, painter, and teacher. Rani looked both excited and intimidated by me, and she considered herself lucky to find such a talented teacher. Looking back, I see I was the lucky one, because my angel agreed to be a part of my life.

We spent many seasons in nature teaching her how to draw. At the same time, Rani fascinated me with her looks. I had fallen in love with her the first day I met her. You know me—I had to play it slow for the next few years as her teacher. I did everything I could to impress her with my skills and design knowledge.

However, I was impatient while I waited for Rani to fall in love with me. I purchased a house near her house so I could spend more time with her, waiting and watching her to grow under my eyes.

During this time, she fell in love with me. And what is love without sex? So, after a few years, we started doing the funny thing called sex. I had to wait for her to grow, because I am not comfortable having an intimate life with one who is not an adult. Rani had a contract to fulfill, the concept of unconditional love, and for a child it is usually tougher to achieve it. And because of that, I prefer to wait. We had plenty of fun together, and I loved her from the bottom of my heart.

After a while, I saw Rani become sad. I demanded to know what happened.

She confessed, "I am pregnant, and I cannot tell to my parents," she confessed. "They won't understand, and they will punish me when they will find out. I don't want to create problems for Daddy, but I don't know what to do."

I replied, "Don't worry, angel. We will get married this month. Do you want to marry me?"

"Yes, I want to marry you. Why have you never asked? In my condition, I cannot refuse you now, even if I do not want you—right?"

Rani was playing with my heart, trying to make me feel guilty. "Let's go and ask your father for permission to get married, and then we can prepare for the wedding," I said. "I purchased a ring for you a long time ago, but I thought, why rush? Our love and passion are bigger than this ring. Do you accept this ring, my love?"

She gave me a long kiss and admired the ring on her finger, then we headed toward her house.

When we arrived there, I asked her father for his permission to marry Rani. I said that we were in love, and that we wanted to live together and have a family. I arranged the wedding quickly, as per her family's demand and traditions.

After the marriage, I arranged to live in the mountains for a few months. She needed a special ambiance to relax, and, in her condition, I preferred to be just two of us, away from civilization. When we came back from the long honeymoon, Rani moved in with me. She was in love, and she appreciated me for her entire life. Rani was extremely happy, and she considered me her angel from God. My love for her was increasing, and then she gave me wonderful twin boys. I took excellent care of them, and I provided for them, fulfilling their hopes and dreams as a parent does.

However, I married many other women during this timeline. Traveling from your planet to mine, I had to miss home often because of work troubles. Rani was conscious that I was in a business venture, and that I would have to skip home sometimes. When she got upset because I had been away from her for longer than expected, I had to figure out something to say, because I couldn't stand seeing her upset. Rani never complained, and that irritated me.

So, I had to go back to my planet and replicate myself. Then, my copy could live with her, helping out more around the house and with our children's education. This copy of me had to be the way Rani wanted, so that I could make her happy.

This copying technology is similar to cloning on your planet. We have had this technology for over three hundred thousand years on my planet, but on your planet, today, cloning is still new. However, back then, it was new on my planet, too. But I had to use it to make my wives happy.

Rani became happy again, and she treated me with love and made me feel as special as a prince, which I guess was a reward for me being home more often. When my copy is happy, I am happy too, because I can experience the same emotions as my copy.

During this lifetime, she never told me that I was not human, but she called me "My lovely angel" many times. Could it be because we married when she was pregnant?

I don't understand humans; why do you make a big issue of everything? Do you presume that I wouldn't take care of Rani, or even that I wouldn't marry her? She carried my baby, for God's sake—with papers or without, I am responsible. Yes, we angels care, but humans need papers and people around them in order to celebrate.

Also, you make too much noise about the sentiment called "love." Love is sacred, love is divine, and love is between two people only. Why do you want to share that moment with your family, neighbours, friends, and so on? I don't know. You are strange, with your weird laws that damage people's lives. My lovely Rani, I was looking for her a long time before she met me, and I waited for her to grow up and fall in love with me. Do you think that I would let her kill herself because of the foolish shame and prejudice that surround your traditions? Should I let her be punished by irresponsible parents who punish love if it is not done in specific ways written in your scriptures or your laws? I do not expect your parents to know what love means, or maybe they have forgotten. They attached rules, regulations, and traditions, just for the sake of feeling good about themselves in the face of others.

To get back to the story, I had to go frequently to my planet to make myself age. That was the only way I could avoid questions from my princess regarding my origins. Many times, I wished to tell her about my origins, but I didn't. One day, I asked Rani how she felt regarding aliens, and she became frightened, so I shut up to make her comfortable.

Our life was wonderful and busy with two noisy kids. At the same time, my copy was bored on your planet, because Rani didn't want to entertain or to go out. She preferred to stay in nature and pursue her hobby as a painter. I played my role as husband and father, but it was boring. I preferred my days to be full of action, which gives me some spice in my life.

Do you see what I had done for my earthly love, just for the privilege of making her happy? I gave up my projects and my agenda many times in that life. I never regretted it, because it was my choice to make Rani happy and to fill her heart with pleasure. Because it was my choice and my pleasure, I would have never traded it for something else.

But, we enjoyed a quiet time together after the kids had grown up and moved in with their wives. Now, I had the pleasure of spending more time with Rani, admiring her artwork. I posted her paintings in an art gallery, and, in no time, she became famous. Rani was delighted and satisfied, because she was making her own money. She always wanted to be active, doing and making something around the house and in our life. I never saw her relaxing. Rani was constantly moving. Me? No—I prefer to lie on the sofa with my favourite drink, and if it's possible, I do not even want to think or talk.

With all of my talents, I couldn't help Rani accomplish her unconditional love experiment. She imposed too many conditions her entire life, which blocked her unconditional love concept. I knew her wish to live the concept of unconditional love is impossible in a conditional world, but she will try it next life and I will be there to help here again.

—Lucifer

5

You and Only You

I know you want another story here. I gave you the title, but not the story, yet. I will tell you a love story with the most amazing life that Ada and I experienced together on your Earth.

This time, I found her in Paris, France. Her name was Louise. Her grace shone brightly in the Paris ballrooms and in the hearts of many lovely men. I wanted to be the one for her, so I tried my chances again. *Will she accept me as her husband?* I wondered. *Is she remembering me again? Will she love me the way I love her?* These were the questions that wouldn't allow me any peace of mind.

So, there I was in Paris, following her around in the streets and trying to talk with her. Not a chance. She couldn't hear my soul crying. She was restless, with so many men around her, and she visited ballrooms, operas, theatres, and music performances on a daily basis.

The week before I had gone to a ballroom party hoping to attract her attention; no luck. I couldn't dance with her. I would have had to wait in line for weeks for her. I had to figure out another way to meet her. So, I waited on the street every day, assuming that she might come for a walk. Besides, it was May now, and the parks and botanical gardens were full of blossoming plants. The strong fragrance of flowers expanded in the air. It might have been a hopeless wish that she would appear in the park that spring, but I remembered from my past lives with her that she loved nature, so I was confident that she would show up here soon.

I was right; after a few days of watching, I saw her walking on the street with one of her girlfriends. So, I said to myself, "Aki, take your chance on her once again." I couldn't lose her, because I might've had to wait a long time before I could catch her again. So, I followed her down the street. She was going toward a nearby park. I loved that. Now was my time to talk with my darling, and maybe I would touch her heart, or I could make her remember me.

It was difficult, however. She refused to talk, and, without looking at me, she said, "Dear, I am sorry, but I do not talk with strangers."

I didn't give up so easily. I followed her. It was not the only lifetime where she had rejected me. I was getting used to her attitudes toward me, but I never gave up on her.

Besides, how stupid would it have been to wait for her for so long, and then have no chance to reach her heart? This was *depressing*, as you humans call it. You know me better—could I let her leave? Not a chance. I was as a buffoon in front of her until she gave up and agreed to meet me the next day in the same place at the same time.

She said, "My name is Louise, and I will not be alone, because I do not know you, and I am sorry that I have to bring my girlfriend with me."

I said, "That's okay. At least I can see you again."

Guess what? She didn't show up next day.

After that, I walked daily in the park, waiting for her until she showed up again. A few days later, she appeared. When I met her again, I wanted it to seem like a coincidence where the circumstances had brought us together again.

I said, "I guess you are my destiny, otherwise I do not see any reason to have met you again."

My observation must have touched her heart, because she started giving me more of her time. Reading so many questions in her eyes, I said to myself, "Oh, baby, I hope you will fall in love with me and spend your entire life with me."

From the park, Louise agreed to go to a nearby restaurant to have lunch with me, where I guess I touched her with my style and manners. She asked why I had followed her. *Wow, she had observed that?*

I said, "I wanted to dance with you last week at the dance hall, but you were booked for weeks."

She laughed and said, "Can you blame me for that?"

"No, you are not to blame. I understand that your charm enchants many men around, but I didn't want to die before speaking to you."

I guess she enjoyed what I said, because she giggled at my comment. It was very pleasant to communicate with her, and she had a light in her eyes that made them brighter. I could guess what that was: curiosity. I believe she liked me, and I had caught her sympathy, so I took my chances and invited her for dinner in my quarters.

I added, "You may bring a girlfriend, if you feel it's necessary."

"Okay, I will come at six this afternoon, if this is okay with you."

Hooray! This was my chance. I was looking good, I was rich, I was smart, and I was in love with her—what else could she look for in a man? Do you think just because I am Lucifer, I knew what she likes, or what pleases her? I don't, so I had to play smart, because I don't want to lose her.

So, I instructed my guys to prepare a dinner and a dream evening for us. They created a unique ambiance to make her feel as special as she was. I asked one of my butlers to stay behind her during dinnertime. I wanted to make sure that everything was perfect, nothing was missing, and that she was well served.

The time ran fast, and she arrived for dinner by herself. Well, that was a big surprise for me, and I had to make sure she was comfortable. My butler opened the door, and he invited her into the library, where I was reading a book. In fact, I was just pretending to read, because I wanted to impress my lovely friend. I invited her to have a seat until the dinner was served. We had a small chat about her lifestyle, parents, boyfriends, and friends. While I asked questions and made conversation, I avoided looking at her, because she gave me butterflies in my stomach, and I couldn't think clearly.

That night, she was wearing a stunning long white dress with light purple and blue on it, which perfectly matched her big eyes. She was searching around, making sure that she was in a safe place, and that nobody was going to attack her. Can you blame her? With her gorgeous looks, men couldn't take their eyes off of her. I acted like a genuine gentleman who wouldn't take advantage of her because I respected women and I loved her. It was my wish to show her that I was a nobleman and that she could count on me, so that I could see her again. I didn't want her to take off and never meet me again during this lifetime. My plan was to marry Louise.

I could not wait for another experiment of achieving unconditional love on planet Earth with her. We had tried many times before, but we had never reached that wonderful level of affection. Now, we would try it again. She was always warm, passionate, unpredictable, dynamic, intense, and when she was in love, she was like a volcano—it was hard to put out the fire. I knew that from my other lives with her. She never changed her personality, because those characteristics were the tools she needed to achieve her concept of unconditional love. She didn't remember that, but I did.

After we chatted in the library, we moved into the salon for a drink before dinner. She became comfortable. I noticed how she reacted very familiar to things around her. I had to gain her trust. I would never violate our relationship, because I had been in love with her for a million years. I couldn't screw that up right now, even though my male instincts aroused every time I was around her. It was tough, but my love for her has no limit—it's bigger than everything I have in the world.

We had the supper together, and then we discussed her life. She opened up and talked about her friends. After a few dates, most of her friends wanted to marry her. Lucky me—she hadn't said yes to any of them. She suggested that they all looked similar and that she was looking for a unique man with distinctive qualities—a special man—even if she wasn't certain what those qualities were, exactly.

Here was my chance. *I am different—can I impress her with that?* I wondered. *I will see how it goes, because I am different from her boyfriends, but she hasn't acknowledged that yet.* My goal was to make her to fall in love with me.

I guess I touched her heart on this first date, because she accepted another date with me without thinking about it too much. For the next date, I invited her over again for dinner in my house. I also asked if she was free during the daytime, because I wanted to meet her more often. I asked to spend more time together, because I wished to know her better. She accepted. *Hooray!* I had touched her heart. I guessed that we would soon have to prepare for marriage.

ᶚ

The next day, we went to a nearby classy restaurant for lunch. She showed up a short time after me. She was late for our date, but I had no complaints, even though I was the one who wanted her now. When I saw her entering the restaurant, my heart began pumping quickly. "Exquisite" is nothing compared to her. She was tall and slim, with long blond hair. She was gorgeous, sensual, sexy, you name it. In her long, light blue dress with darker blue accents, she was brighter than a star. I had to behave like a gentleman. It was difficult, but I did it. She was well known in the restaurant, and men gathered around her like bees to honey. That was excellent for me, as I needed time to recover from my excitement.

Louise rushed past the men and came straight to my table as fast as she could. She gave me a big smile as well as an explanation for being late, stating, "Because it's noon, I met many friends on the street. They all wanted to talk and they invited me to have lunch together, so it was hard for me to get here more quickly."

"It is okay, my dear. I have time on my side, so no worries."

While I helped her take a seat at the table, I asked for a waitress to stay next to her during lunchtime. I wanted to be sure that she was comfortable and properly served.

Everything was perfect. She asked me who I was, where I lived, what I did for a living, and other similar questions. She had tried the night before to question me, but I had redirected the discussion toward her lifestyle. Now, I had to answer. "I live far away from France on a small island. When I am not working, I want to enjoy quiet time without the noise of big cities. Most of my time I spend in the mountains, where I have a successful business, which has made me wealthy."

She was attentive to everything I said. While contemplating my true love, she gave me a big, sweet smile that made me dizzy.

I continued, "I am on vacation right now, and I am searching for a nice lady to get married to. It is my time to settle down and have a family and kids. I am fascinated by your charm, and when I attended the ballroom last week, I said to myself, 'This woman has to be my spouse,' because I fell in love with you the first moment I saw you."

She fixed me with her big eyes and then smiled with satisfaction. While I was admiring her, she made me feel timid and wonderful at the same time. I was again intimidated by her grace and charm. I tried not to look at her.

"Since then, I can't stop thinking of you," I said. "When God sent you in my direction in the park once again, I realized this might be my destiny. I had to talk to you. I didn't want to wait for the next ballroom. You might have been booked for weeks, and I wouldn't have been able to meet you. I tried to talk with you last week, but you refused me from the beginning. I didn't give up on you, so I insisted until you promised me a date the next day. The following day, I waited for you a few hours, but you didn't show up to our date. While I tried to forget you and your grace, destiny put us face to face again in the park. Because I have no time to search for women, I tried my luck with you again. If you do not want my presence, let me know, because I want to meet you daily. I want to spend more time together, to see if there exists a spark of love between us."

Smiling, she said, "Darling, I enjoy your personality because you differ from the other men I date. It would be my pleasure to meet you daily while you're on vacation. I cannot fall in love so rapidly, but I love your company. Also, I recognize you from somewhere, but it is difficult to know from where, exactly. I cannot be so sure."

"Your appearance is familiar too, but I do not recall that we've ever met. For the past three years, I worked in the mountains, and I met no women."

She stared at me for a long time, and then replied, "That's weird, because my recollection is that I met you a long time ago, but this sounds impossible, as you suggest."

I hoped she did not remember me from the other side of the veil. That mustn't be true, otherwise it could have ruined our relationship—or make it better. Who could know?

I was different than her friends, and my face was familiar to her. Would this make me a winner again? Hooray! Perhaps I would have her love soon, but I did not want to rush in so fast. I did not want to marry her if she did not fall in love with me. If she did not fall in love, we could not achieve the unconditional love experience she was running after in this lifetime. Remember, the wish she had was to experience unconditional love. She didn't remember or recall it, but I did.

We left the restaurant together, and I escorted her home. She radiated delight, happiness, and joy.

We met a few times, and I hadn't even kissed her yet. It was the toughest part of my relationship with her. I informed her, a few times, that I was in love with her. It was strange, but *love*, for me, is sacred. I prowled until the time was right for her to become my wife. Wouldn't you do the same? I didn't want to lose her, because I was in love with her. I had to wait for her to fall in love with me, and then we would decide together what to do.

Another day, we were in front of her house, and I reminded her about having dinner at my place that night. I noticed she was jubilant and satisfied. In the meantime, she was looking me up and down. She comforted me with a big happy smile on her face and promised to come in time for dinner. She left radiating joy, satisfaction, pleasure, and delight, and I was feeling in my heart that she appreciated me. I was burning hard inside, and my heart was crying with happiness. My love for her was intense, and I had to stop myself from kissing her. I said to myself, "I must kiss her tonight." How long do you think I could have endured just waiting for her to give me a sign? I had to take my chances again. Now she knew me, and I was confident that I had captured her interest, otherwise she wouldn't waste time with me.

I went home and prepared for the evening. Time passed slowly when she wasn't around me, and it flew by when she was.

At five p.m., she showed up wearing an impressive gray dress that made her glow in the sunset. I was in the garden. I saw her coming, and I rushed toward her. We had a tour of the garden, and I tried to kiss her. She expected that, because she kissed me back. Hooray! It was my first kiss with my beloved friend on this timeline. Even now, I can feel her lips on my lips.

We had a nostalgic walk in the garden, played a few games together, kissed more, and after that, we went into the house for supper. Here, I played it cool to make her comfortable. I sensed she was not ready yet for a full relationship. Well, you know me—I wasn't in a rush to do something stupid. Destroying what we had started wasn't in my plans, so I acted like a trustworthy man again. I kept my distance, just in case she wanted to get closer, but she became serious and relaxed, as though nothing had happened in the garden. We had a quiet supper, and then we listened to music and danced together.

Oh! She was an excellent dancer. I messed up a few times, but she pretended not to notice. I dared to kiss her again, and she accepted it. I realized that she had expected it, but I might have been mistaken. With women, I never know what to expect, and I never try to understand. If, in one case, she might agree, in another case she might refuse, but this didn't happen. She said she liked to kiss me because I was a great kisser, so I kissed her more. After dinner, we went into the garden, sat on the bench, and talked about subjects such as music, literature, and other things. Thank God that I had knowledge about the arts. I switched the discussion toward love, and she sensed a strong love coming to her from me.

Oh, mama, she had good perception, so I couldn't hide it anymore. I told her again, "I fell in love with you when I met you the first time at the dance hall."

She giggled with pleasure as I kissed her again, and then she kissed me back with enthusiasm and passion. I didn't want to go further at that time, so I asked her if she wanted me to walk her home because it was getting late. I guess she hadn't foreseen that, so she kissed me again. After a while, she mentioned that it would be a pleasure if I escorted her home. I guess I confused her, but it was better this way. It was not my plan to do something in a hurry, or to force her into my arms. When I'm falling in love, I am like a hurricane.

So, imagine this: I'm a hurricane, and she's a volcano. That's a good reason to stop it. No time for mistakes here. She would have enough time to fall in love with me later. When we arrived at her house, she invited me inside to meet her parents.

I said, "Dear, in the morning I have to leave, and I do not have time now to meet your parents. But I will be glad to meet them next time I am in town."

She was paralyzed because of the news, and she asked, "Are you ever coming back?"

I replied, "Yes, I love you, and I'll come back in a week to spend more time with you." She was disappointed, but she didn't show it—I could just read her feelings from a distance.

I left the planet next morning, and I planned to stay away for more than one week. Why, you ask? I had to check if she is in love with me or if she had any affection for me. I was in love, and it would be hard to stay away from her, even for an hour, but I had no choice. In the meantime, I had to prepare a few things and arrange my future with her.

After three weeks, I came back to Paris and tried to talk to her. I found out that she hadn't gone out from her house for the past three weeks, and she had seen nobody. When I spoke with somebody from her house, he said Louise was sad and depressed and that she didn't want to talk to anybody. What do you think that means? For me, that meant she was in love. I left a message for her, asking her on a dinner date tomorrow at five in the afternoon. If she didn't agree, she could send me a note.

I received not a word from her, so I showed up to her door at five the next day. She was dressed for our date, and she was heartbroken, but still gorgeous. I asked if she wanted to go to my place, or to a restaurant. Whatever she wanted. She said that was not important. *Well, this looks tougher than I expected,* I thought. *She is upset, and she does not ask me questions, so I have to ask questions.*

"How did you spend your time, my lady, while I was in the mountains?"

She complained, claiming that never in her life had this happened to her. After my departure, she had felt alone and unhappy. When she saw that I didn't return in a week, she became worried that something had happened. She asked why I hadn't delivered a letter informing her that I would be late.

I said, "It was not possible, because I was in the mountains, and I had more complications than I expected. I was busy, and even if

I could send a note from there, the message would arrive after me."

I apologized for my late return. She accepted my explanation and became more comfortable again. I kissed her and told her that I had missed her while I was away from Paris. Her face became brighter right away, and her eyes shone of delight, and she placed a smile on her face.

What do you think? Was I right with my intentions to make her wait longer? Now I knew she was in love with me, even if she would never say it in this timeline. I would have her love and her heart again.

I told her, "My darling I am in love with you, and I want to marry you if you will fall in love with me."

I explained to her my business, and I specified that she might have to move to live with me on my island. If she didn't want to, I would buy a castle for her here in France, but I would miss my home. She radiated love through the entire room, and she told me she wanted both.

I asked, "What do you mean by both—getting married, staying in Paris, or going to my island? There are three elements involved."

I understood what she meant, but I liked to play with her a little. I wanted to discover her thoughts regarding marriage, because I wanted to make sure that we were on the same page. In the meantime, I asked her to specify if she wanted to get married this month, or if she wanted to wait. I was looking at her, because she was becoming uncomfortable again. I guess I had put too much pressure on her, considering what she had gone through during the time I was away.

Not knowing if she understood me, I took my chances again. I took the ring from my pocket and asked for her hand in marriage. This came as a surprise for her, because she laughed out loud, gave me a kiss, and said yes. I put the ring on her finger, and she kissed me with intensity. Maybe I could have had her that night, but I wanted to wait and examine her attitude. After that, we had dinner together. Afterwards, we moved into the living room for a chat. I asked her again: Paris or my island.

She said, "It would be a pleasure for me to have them both, my dear." This is what she had meant with her earlier answer.

I inquired once again, "When do you want to get married?"

She amazed me, because she answered, "Now!"

I knew what she meant by that, but I preferred not to show her that I had understood.

I added, "Okay, if you prefer now, let's meet your parents and ask for your hand in marriage."

She replied, "Okay, but not now—let's do that tomorrow. You can come have supper with my family."

"That will be wonderful," I responded. "So I will show up tomorrow evening, and I will take you home now. What do you think, my love?"

As I watched her, she became uncomfortable again. She preferred to spend more time with me, but she didn't mention that. I was excited, and my mind was occupied by a tremendous passion for her. What could I say? I was the happiest man on planet Earth. I felt like getting her into my arms and never letting her leave. Yes, I wished that, but I let her go home that night, because my passion for her was bigger than my male instincts.

The next day, I arrived at her house later in the afternoon. She introduced me to her parents. I took my chances, and I asked her father, who seemed like a nice guy, to chat with me. While we talked, he was interested in knowing more about me, my life, and my sentiments for Louise. So, we went out to the terrace for a drink, and I opened the discussion of my marriage with Louise.

"Dear Philip, I am here to ask for your daughter's hand in

marriage. Most of my time I live in the mountains and on my island. I am a wealthy man, because I am in the business of extracting gold from mountains."

Philip replied, "Where did you come from, Aki? I never heard your name around here in France. Who are you? Do you have any feelings for my daughter? What about your wealth? Are you in a financial position to take care of Louise?" He was interested more in my wealth than my love for Louise. Phillip looked comfortable, with his big house and servants. He was a wealthy man, but he was interested in his daughter being very wealthy. So, hooray! I met that requirement, thank God.

I told him of my arrangements with his daughter, and how much I loved her. When I mentioned that she would be the richest woman on the planet, I touched his heart and he blessed our marriage.

He replied, "Louise accepted your ring, so I guess we should prepare for the wedding."

He looked at me, gave me a big smile, and slapped me friendly on the shoulder.

I said, "Philip, I am the one who will prepare the wedding the way she wants, so don't worry. I will organize and pay for everything."

While planning for the wedding, I searched for a castle, as per Louise's wish. His father wanted to take part with wedding expenses, but I refused him.

I informed him, "Philip, I am in love with your gorgeous daughter, and in this marriage, I want to cover her in diamonds, so I have to do that by myself."

He acknowledged this and then said, "Aki, I want to know if you need any financial help."

"Okay!" I replied. "If I need any help, I will tell you."

I ordered my tailor to assemble a wedding gown for Louise—the most extravagant one that had ever existed, packed with pearls, gems, and diamonds. Her dress had to be fabulous as per her wish. But hey, I was rich, and I had my dream princess.

Soon, my guys found a castle for us to move into after the wedding. They got the architect working on restoring the castle so that we would be happy there. Louise wanted to decorate the castle by herself, so I let her take care of that job while I arranged the wedding. She wanted a big wedding with all of her friends there on the happiest day of her life. I told her to call the whole of Paris if she wanted. She smiled again, and then gave me a long kiss for accepting her wish. I would have loved something else, but I was waiting for her to be ready.

To go back to my life, I preferred to invest most of my time with my lovely Louise, but it was not possible on this timeline. I had to travel back and forth, in to and out of the planet with my business. Because of that, I prepared a smart plan. I would tell her that we are going to visit my island for the honeymoon. Once there, she would see my workplace on my planet. My plan was to take her home with me. I did not think I could live without her, and I hoped she would accept my plan to spend some time on my island.

I did not actually have an island, but I had to invent a story for her. It wasn't hard to get an island, but I had to prepare her for something different than what she was used to seeing. If I had to buy an island, I could quickly develop something there, but I didn't want that. I wondered what she would think of the fake island, and how she would feel being with me in the mountains on my planet.

When I had her over for the next supper, I brought this to the table to explain my position. I told her that if she didn't want to, she still had time to cancel the wedding. I do not know what I would have done if she'd cancel the wedding, because I was badly in love with her. I guess I am lucky because she giggled again, gave me a kiss, and said that she wanted to be engaged with my work and help me with my business. Hooray! I had an apprentice now. She was fabulous, and this was more than I expected from her.

In three months, we stole each other's hearts and got married. I didn't know her that well, but I would take Louise for our honeymoon to my planet.

I was wondering what she would think of my island. Over there, everything is strange; we even wander around by flying. Imagine having to explain this. I was curious about how my idea would work out. If she created problems, I would have to get back to Paris and reside in our castle, just to make her happy, as a backup plan.

After the wedding—where she was better looking than a queen, because she was *my* queen—we had to stay overnight in our castle. Wow—I had waited for such a long time to set off fireworks together, and finally the time had arrived.

The next day, I prepared her for the journey to the island—which meant another planet, but she didn't know that. So, we packed and headed out of this planet. I had to switch to many different transportation vehicles in order to encourage her to become tired and sleep. The flight to my planet was shorter than an hour.

When we arrived at the destination, I placed Louise on the bed next to me. I loved staring at her, and I admired her charm until she woke up and opened her big, wide eyes. I woke up my darling with a kiss. She asked if we had reached the destination.

I said, "Yes, we are home." She was so stunning. I still keep her image in my heart, even today. I kissed her and we had an interesting, lovely night together. The next day she woke up before me and ran out to see the so-called island.

She asked, "Where is this place?"

"This is Paradise Island," one of my guys answered.

"This is Paradise Island."

"Wow, this place *looks* like a paradise, and I cannot believe I am a part of it." Louise came back into the bedroom. She kissed me all over to wake me up and begged me to go out with her to visit the Paradise Island.

I asked, "Which Paradise Island?"

She answered, "Your Island! Aren't we here now?"

I realized that my guys must have told her that to make her happy. I said, "Louise, everything on my island will be very different than what you are used to and what you experienced in Paris."

"Darling, I am fascinated by your place. It is so extraordinary here—more so than anything I've ever known—and this delights me the most, and I love it. Can I visit your workplace today, my love?"

Can you imagine that? Who could foresee that she would be so enthusiastic about her new place in the universe, and so happy about living outside France? I worried because I didn't want to stay away from her for too long on my planet, but in the end, everything worked out perfectly.

Now, to make the story short, she loved my planet, which she understood was an island far away from Paris—around twenty hours. She became involved with my work, and she came up with recommendations for developing our technologies. She had a wild imagination, and I told my guys to do everything she thought of while she lived there. I was fortunate to have her in my life again.

It was the first life she spent with me that she didn't question my origins. She accepted everything in this lifetime with gratitude, and she took into consideration other people's welfare. She came up with the idea to produce and sell our technology in Europe, because they were behind us in technology.

"This is a great idea, my love," I replied. "I will investigate how we can carry out this technology to work for humanity."

Well, she had shocked me again with how easy and comfortable she seemed, living on my planet as she had been born there. My guys loved her very much, and they made her feel admired and loved.

⁊

Time passed quickly, and she brought us two nice sons. Our boys looked like her and not much like me, but I was pleased about that. They were living on my planet, and they occasionally came to Earth.

We lived a joyful life together, but again we didn't carry out unconditional love in the third dimension. I sold the castle in Paris, because she didn't want to stay there. We came into Paris a few times per year to visit her parents, and we lived with them during our stays there.

Louise loved living on my planet. She never acknowledged that it wasn't Earth. She got caught up in my work, especially my responsibilities, so I let her help me with my job. So, in this life, I achieved little with my work—she took everything from me.

There were a few parts of my work that she never knew about. When she by chance noticed projects that were destructive to people's lives, she got in my face and questioned me. She played her charm, promising me another kid if I wouldn't apply that technology, because it might disrupt people's lives. These were warfare programs, and methods of conquering other realms and dimensions. She thought that we were still on Earth and that I was going to apply the new technology on other humans. So, I had to delay most of my projects, but I enjoyed being with her. She amazed me with her intuition and perceptions of things.

Many times, I wanted to tell her the truth about our place, but I couldn't foresee how she would react. I thought that maybe I should talk about other lives on other planets, or about life after death, or maybe her project on Earth to find unconditional love. I had to shut up, and I said nothing; my life with her was more important than telling the truth. Somehow, I didn't have enough courage to tell her.

Now, I regret this, but what's the point in living in the past? It won't help. I should just move on to another love story about her—one where I can remember just the great times we spent together, and then enjoy them for the rest of my eternity.

—Lucifer

6

Somewhere in Time

Dear Ada,

It is about time to show you another life, one where you were abused by your family. You were part of a big family with four brothers. The part of the world where you were born was not proper for female life, packed with exploitation and controlling husbands. Your family was very modest, and men exploited their wives, and women had no rights in that society.

I sought you in my glass technology because I knew you had picked up a body, and I found you right away. You never left your village, and you had no clue how wonderful the world was outside your region. You were ten years old, and your dad was harming you on a daily basis. Your mom couldn't say a word, because her spouse would beat her, too; she was a very unhappy woman with no rights in her house. Her intention was to take you and leave her husband. In the meantime, she was frightened that he might find out and murder you both. Because of that, she delayed her plan and searched for a family who desired help around the house. She wished to find a job for you—a job far away from the house and your father's harm.

When I realized what life you had, I had to run to save you. I contacted your mother and talked with her. We had to arrange this without your father noticing. Together, we made your departure look like it was his decision, not hers.

It wasn't easy contacting your mother, because of her dominating husband. After a while, I found her, we talked for a few minutes, and together we arranged for your departure from her house. I accepted what your mother advised, and I visited your father. Early in the morning the next day, I knocked at your father's door. When your father opened the door, I said, "Sir, I need help in my house, and I found that out you have an inexperienced girl and wish to offer her a job."

Your father replied, "I have four boys that need jobs, too."

"Right now, I need just a youthful girl to take care of the dog and to help my housekeeper," I answered. "My housekeeper is too old to work in the house by herself, and she needs help."

Your father decided right away to let you leave—that is, if I offered him a sum of money. I detest paying for my love, but I had no choice. I had to pay the price that your father demanded. For me, you are valuable because you are on my list every time you get a human body. Besides, you are more precious than everything I have.

During the negotiation time, I mentioned to your father that I lived in Europe, and that I would get you there. I said, "There will be no chance for you, sir, to see your girl again in this lifetime, nor speak with her, unless you come to Europe."

This didn't disturb him, and he proposed better payment and said adieu. I never noticed a trace of regret in his eyes.

After we completed the details of your departure, your dad called your mom. She turned around quickly and asked him how she could help.

Your dad replied, "Arrange our daughter, for she is moving to Europe with this gentleman. He has a job for her there."

Your mother was so pleased with the decision that she could barely refrain from showing her happiness. She introduced me to you, and she said, "You are going with this man. He has a job for you, and you will live with him. He is a good man, so don't be afraid, my darling."

She gave you a long kiss and wished you good luck and happiness in your life. I was impressed with your mother in this emotional scene. She cried because she knew that she would never see you again. In the meantime, she was radiating with happiness as she watched you go. When I had talked to her, she had begged me to find a place for her little girl, and to help her get you out from your parents' house.

As we left together on our long drive to Europe, I looked at you. You were shy, and I felt the fear of the unknown coming out from you. As I was looking at you, I saw a young girl with her entire face covered in bruises from the beatings she had received from her father. You destroyed my heart when I saw you in this state. I tried to chat with you, but you were shy, and instead of answering my questions, you just nodded your head.

Oh well, I thought. The poor girl—why she chose such a life for herself, I don't understand. From no one, I will make her the happiest girl on the planet.

Because you chose not to talk, I asked you to sleep, because the way home was long and you needed to relax. In the beginning, you didn't want to sleep, but after a while you did. I took you in my arms and put you comfortably on the bench, and then I covered your body with a blanket. Because the way back home was long by carriage, we had to sleep in hotels during our travel home.

When we stopped in the first city, I bought a few nice pieces of clothing for you. You were very happy looking at your clothes, and when we arrived at the hotel, I asked for a doctor to heal your bruises.

You received my attention each day, and you became comfortable around me. I knew that you didn't know another language, so we chatted for a while in your own language. I knew many languages, so it was not a problem for me.

After you tried on the dresses I had bought, you came toward me, kissed my hand, and said, "Thank you."

This shocked me, and I told you that you didn't have to do this gesture in future. I said, "You must not be afraid of me, because I will never abuse you as your father did, and I will never hit you. With me, you will have a nice quiet life full of attention and love."

You pulled back a few steps. You hadn't known that your mother had told me more about you, and you cried.

I continued, "You are lucky, because I was looking for a girl like you to help me around the house. I will always treat you with respect and love. I respect my employees, and I help them with what they need. You will have doctors check your health from time to time. Besides, I will give you an income, so you can buy what you want. I want you to have an education, because your parents couldn't afford that. Don't make such big eyes at me, because I will pay for it. If you want to learn more, I will pay for everything.

"I know your story from your mother. She loves you very much, and she planned to run away from home with you. When I met your mother, she said that she wanted to save her little girl, and that she needed to find somebody to help her. She didn't want to lose you, but she had no choice. You and your life were precious to her. I proposed to your mother that I take you with me. She agreed right away. She will miss her little girl, and she will pray to God to help you.

"Your mother wanted for you to live a better life than you had at home. So, she told me to contact your father, and I paid him to take you with me. I do not want to buy girls, but your mother was desperate with your situation and with your father's rules. She wanted to help *you stay away from home and away from your father.*

"Now, my little one, you know that I know everything about you from your mother. You owe this to your mother. She was crying and imploring me to help her little girl. Just because I gave your father money for you, it doesn't mean I own you, or that you are my slave. I want you to understand that I will be a real father to you—a father that loves his child. So be happy, my sweet girl, because from now on you will live your life in joy. Your name will be 'Mona,' from now on, because we live in Paris, and your name is hard to pronounce."

In a week, we arrived at the destination. You looked tired and sleepy, so I asked my guys to prepare you a room. In a few days, I filled your room with toys and books, and I hired teachers for your education. The time passed quickly, and you looked adorable as the bruises went away. In the new dresses that I had bought, you looked like a young princess.

Under my eyes, you received the teachings you needed. You learned piano as well as a few languages, such as French and English. You had a bright mind, and the teachers loved you. Time kept passing, and you easily learned how to play piano and other instruments. During our evenings together, you would play the piano for me and entertain me with your wonderful voice. I was waiting for you to grow up. My plan was to make you to fall in love with me and to marry me when you grew older.

After ten more years, my girl was well educated and living a luxury life in my house. She looked gorgeous, smart, and intelligent. She was talented, and she never asked anything about her parents. I did not think she missed them—in fact, I believe she'd forgotten them. Now, as she was getting older, I was watching her as a lover, not as a father. I was trying to develop ideas how to make her fall in love with me. This was not an easy task, believe me. Until now, I had acted as her father, but I want to switch that to a husband. If I asked her to marry me, she would say "yes." She remembered her early years with her natural parents, and she thought she belonged to me because I bought her. I did not want her to feel so low and marry me because she felt she owed me.

One night, after we had played piano and a few funny games, I told her, "Tomorrow, I have to leave the city for one week. I hope you will not get bored while I will be away. If you want to see friends or have a party, you are free to have one party at home."

She said, "It's not necessarily fun when you are away."

I specified, "Whilst I am gone, you are the boss in the house. You can visit the neighbours, or you can do whatever pleases you."

She looked shocked by the news. I never stayed away from her and the house for that long. She gave me a forced smile, and then she said that she would be okay. I sensed a little emotion there, as if I would leave her forever, but she didn't say anything. I promised that I would come sooner if I finished the job faster.

I woke up early the next morning, and then I went into her room and kissed her forehead. She was sleeping, and she didn't hear or feel me. It wasn't easy to leave her for even an hour, but I had to see if I had feelings for her. I wanted to see where we stood in this timeline.

જ

I couldn't stay away for one week, so I came back in four days. She was so happy to see me. I had gotten a few gifts for her, and I saw how happy she looked, as if she was a kid again. *Oh, my darling, how can I tell you how much I love you and how I am waiting for you to grow up and be my wife?* I thought. I couldn't say that to her, so I tried another strategy. I asked her if she had any boyfriends, because now she was growing up. She said that she was not interested in any man that she had met.

I said, "Okay, I understand that you are too young to get married, but it is time to maybe have a boyfriend. What do you think, my darling?"

"You are the only man that I am interested in, because I love you, and you are the only one I will date and marry."

That was a shock for me. Now I was the one in the middle, and she was watching *me* from the side to see my reaction. I was shaking with happiness. I asked her if she had any feelings for me besides daughter feelings. She said that she had loved me since the day that I had taken her from her parents. She had made a promise to herself to marry me when she grew up, if I wanted her. She never dared to tell me this, because I would have considered her still a kid.

Well, it was easy again, because I didn't have contenders. I did not want to marry Mona without making her fall in love with me. So, I planned a vacation for both of us. She was pleased to go on the vacation with me. I planned to go to a nice place with a lake, where we could relax and start from the beginning. I found a great place in the mountains close to a lake. It was a hot summer, and the mountain-fresh air would add a romance to our relationship.

I knew what she was like from her previous lives. Also, I knew of her contract to find unconditional love on planet Earth. Of course, she didn't know that, but this relationship was not going to get her the achievement of an unconditional love. I tried my best to help her meet that goal.

The next day, we were headed toward mountains early in the morning. We arrived there around six in the evening, and the air was refreshing and filled with the nice fragrance of the flowers around the house.

I looked at her, and I asked, "Are we getting two rooms or one?" She said, "One!"

Hooray! What do you think of that? So, I rented a suite with one bedroom and living room. When we entered the room, she was shocked upon seeing two rooms, but I didn't say a word. I looked at her, and she looked uncomfortable again.

I said to her, "My darling, you will take the bedroom, and I will sleep here in the living room." She looked at me from the top to the bottom and then came to me, smiling. She took my hand and kissed it, while looking into my eyes. I looked at her, and she was crying.

I asked, "What is it, my princess?"

"You don't love me, and it is hard for me to go through life without you being my husband. I am in love with you, but I don't know how to tell you."

Now I was uncomfortable too, because I didn't expect her to be so sincere and innocent. I took her head in my palms and I gave her a kiss. She kissed me back.

I told her that I had fallen in love with her a long time ago, but that I had waited for her to be ready for the long run. I didn't want to rush her into anything. It was very hard for me to go through this life without her being my wife, as well. She was pleased with my answer, and she covered me in kisses so that I couldn't talk anymore. I had been waiting for this fiery passion with her, and I was prepared for this event. So, I took my position on one knee, and then I took her hand, kissed it, and asked for her hand in marriage.

She laughed, and she said, "Yes!"

I put a ring on her finger, and I looked at her face. She looked more gorgeous than ever, and she was asking, "Aki, why do you choose me as your wife?"

Oops! That was hard to answer, but I had to figure out something to say. I tried getting some time to think about what to answer, and I asked her to play something on the piano. While she was admiring her ring on her finger, she went to the piano and started playing romantic music. I got close to her and kissed her on the shoulder while she was playing. She turned to me and started kissing me with passion. I moved her into the bedroom, and she was looking at me, and asked me again, "Aki, why do you want to marry me?"

I said, "I am going to tell you tomorrow, because right now I want to enjoy this moment."

She giggled, and we had the first night together—just us with our passionate love and our hearts beating as one.

The next day came and I had to answer to her question. Why did I want to marry her? *What a question*, I was asking myself. Why do I go after her every time she gets a new human body? I do not think I knew why. I knew that I loved her very much unconditionally on the other side of the veil. I behaved like I was competing for her hand all the time with other men, every time she got a human body. I had promised her that I would show up in her lifetimes and help her out with her experiments.

Surely, this was not the only reason why I had shown up in her life over and over again. I was really in love with her on the other side of the veil. But I think this was the only reason that I bothered her on all her lifetimes. Besides that, I had promised to help her with her contract of finding and experiencing unconditional love on planet Earth.

Therefore, I had to think of an answer that would not make her think or bother her in any way. So, I said, "My darling, I already told you this story ten years ago. Because you were young, maybe you forgot. I was in your town when your mother caught me, and she begged me to take you from your parents' home and save you from your father's abuses. At the time, I never considered how beautiful and smart you are—I just promised your mom that I would help you. I have always liked helping the people around me, so this was why I jumped in to help you.

"When your mother started crying and kept begging me to help, I couldn't resist. I promised that I would put an end to your pain and misery, and that I would take you with me. She knew that she would never see you again, but her love for you was bigger than the desire to see you. So, I took you with me in the carriage that day, as per your mother's wish. Although you were covered in bruises, I noticed how beautiful you were, and that gave me an unexplainable thrill. I wondered how a girl so beautiful could live such a tragic life at home.

"This was not the time that I fell in love with you. Do you remember the party that we had for your birthday, when you were seventeen years old? I was hiding in a corner of the room, and I was looking at you. All the men were admiring you, and they stayed in line to dance with you and kiss your hand. A few men told me that they wanted to be the contenders for your hand when you were ready to date; they were waiting for you to get older and become ready to wed. This was the moment when I invited you to dance with me. You quickly rejected all the other men, just to dance with me. That was impressive. It was a very romantic song, and you left yourself in my hands to lead you. You threw me a look full of love and questions. You were wearing a pink and white dress that accentuated all of your form and beauty. In that moment, you pierced through my heart, and suddenly I had fallen in love with you.

"Of course, I didn't show you this, because you loved me as a father. I imagined all the time that I would be marrying you, because my life without you in it does not make sense. I was afraid of your suitors, since they started coming to me to ask my consent to woo you. I watched to see if you spent more time with any guy. I wished that you would not like or want any of them. I prayed to God for you to love me the way I love you. When men came to visit you, I was always worried that I would lose you. When I was gone for four days and I said 'Have fun and organize a party at my house,' to be honest with you, I was afraid. I feared that I might lose you, but I never wanted to force you to marry me.

"My love for you has grown for the past couple years. I wanted you to fall in love with me as I had with you, and to look at me the way I looked at you. I could not spend my days with a person who married me for my money or out of obligation, not love. Great was my surprise when you told me that you do not like any man but me. Then you gathered the courage to tell me how you felt. I am glad we both feel the same."

I had to stop talking, because she was kissing me again. I continued, "I understand that your love for me was not necessarily because I helped you to escape from your family. Also, I understand that I am the kind of man whom you accept and expect, because I meet all the qualities that you appreciate in a man. Believe me, I am proud to be chosen. At the same time, you make me feel like the luckiest and happiest man on the planet. Here and now, I promise to make you the happiest woman in the universe. I know your pleasures, sorrows, and desires, because I have taken care of you since you were young. For all of this time, I have held you close to my heart. I had to make sure you were not missing anything that your heart desired. Now that you know the truth about me, when did you start to fall in love with me, really?"

I started be unable to find words while talking to her, because she was watching me, with her eyes full of admiration and pleasure. I was getting goosebumps and shocks when I watched her. I had to direct the discussion to her by asking questions; this was always my way out. As you can see, I am not that good with women; they always freeze me with shock. Before she answered, she took my head in her tiny hands and started to kiss me passionately.

Women have their own innate talents for paralyzing men when they are in love with them. In all my life, I've never been paralyzed by a man, but I've never been able to resist a woman when I've fallen in love with her. I guess all the men out there understand what I am talking about. We all have been there, falling for the one in our life.

Now, let me return to my story. I think my story left a deep impression on her heart. She was lying on the sofa, and she put her head on my lap. She began to tell me what she had felt since I took her from parents' house.

"First, I want to tell you that I have never forgotten my mother, and what she did out of love for me. I would have liked very much to see her, but I never wanted to meet my father again. When I left with you, I began to pray to God not to be beaten again. I could not endure it anymore. Then, I saw you looking at me with a lot of pain in your heart. I was covered with bruises, and from that moment I knew that I was in good hands, and that you were not like my father. We were in the hotel when you called the doctor. Then, I understood that you would treat me with respect and love. I thank God that He finally heard my cries of pain, and that He put me in the hands of a man who cares about me. I repeated this to myself many times.

"The life that I was starting then could not be worse than the one I had in my parents' house. That gave me confidence and trust in you. With each passing day, I noticed your concern for me, and your respect and admiration for all I was doing. I always thought that whenever I was ready to find a man, he must be like you: gentle, understanding, caring, and loving. Time passed, and many men started to surround me with their desires of winning my heart. Whenever I was invited to a dinner or a date, I always checked the men to see if they had any of your qualities. So far, nobody has, so I had to keep rejecting them after the first date. My man has to be like a superman—which is the way that I see you. He has to be meek, he has to fall in love with me, and I to fall in love with him. I couldn't fall in love with any of the men I dated, because I kept comparing them to you.

"I was in love with you more than them, but I didn't know where you stood. Do you look at me as your kid, or do you look at me as your girlfriend and future wife? I began to wonder what was wrong with me, because I didn't want to see or get to know another man. They all had good intentions, and they wanted to get to know each other better. I was the one who felt that something was missing, and I refused them. My eyes and my mind were always headed toward you, with great love.

"I began to not sleep well, and I couldn't get you out of my heart and head. I was thinking and always praying that our relationship could be more than a father-and-daughter-type connection. In fact, you never signed any adoptive papers, so I am not your child on paper. I always wondered if it was possible to make you fall in love with me and marry me. You didn't give me any sign that you might like me as a wife or girlfriend, so I took my chances, and kissed you first. I was already over twenty years old, and I didn't want to wait any longer for you to take the first step. I wanted to see if there was anything for me in your heart. I was amazed by how prepared you were to marry me.

"I think we have loved each other for a long time. You had to wait because of my age, and we both stuck around for the right time to bring it to the table. I often wondered why you never had any woman. Did you hide them from me, or did you never have any women? I was looking at you, and I was wondering how a man so cute, rich, and good looking as you had no woman in his life.

"Now that you know my secret, I wish to let you know that I love you passionately, and I have for a long time. I am pleased to continue this beautiful relationship as husband and wife. You are the ideal man for me, so there is no need to put me through the tests again. You left me alone for four days, and I understood why. I was sad during this period, because instead of telling me what was in your heart, you preferred to flee from me. I knew that you had no other woman, because I never saw one beside you. I do not understand why you left, but I am glad that you came back to me.

"Now that I have agreed to be your wife, I would like to invite my parents to our wedding, if you do not mind, and if it's possible. Now, you can sleep comfortably, because you have my heart forever."

Oh, my God, I don't think I could have gotten an answer more pleasant than this. I knew that I was her guardian angel, as she had told me many times. I did not expect to become her husband so quickly and so easily.

Usually, our past lives had been full of battles between me and other men who wanted her hand. I always needed time to get the skills required to make her fall in love with me. I could now say that I was in the ninth heaven. I was joyful, and I was the happiest man on Earth.

I sent the news to Mona's parents, and I invited them to the wedding. After two weeks, I got an answer from her mother. She said that she would be happy to come to the wedding. She missed her little girl a lot, but she could not afford the journey. Her husband and two boys had died, and the other two boys were married with kids, but they didn't have money for this travel, either.

I told Mona the news from home, and she asked me to do something to get her mother to come and live with us. Of course, she used all her charms to make me fulfill her wish. I knew she was spoiled, because that's the way I'd raised her—spoiled and lacking nothing.

Do you think I could refuse her anything? No, so I had to take care of the immigration papers for her mother, as well as her brothers with their families—I thought I should surprise her by bringing her brothers, too. I noticed that she hadn't asked me to pay for her brothers to come to our wedding. Later, she did ask me how much it would cost to bring them over. I guess she didn't have the money saved to pay for their travel.

A few weeks later, I purchased two houses close to us for her brothers. Because they had families, it would be better for them to live by themselves. As for her mother, I decided to keep her with us. She was getting older and had some heath issues, and Mona missed her so much. Besides, our house was big enough to offer a roof to all of us. If she didn't like living with us, I would get something for her that was close to our house.

I sent a letter to her mother to prepare herself for her immigration to Paris, along with her boys and their families. The wedding day was almost three months away. It was enough time to bring them over and to finish the documents and arrange for their travel.

After two months, I had finished all legal formalities that humans use to bring their families closer to them. It was going to be a big surprise for Mona to see her entire family. I couldn't wait to see her reaction when she found out that they would all be living in Paris forever. I had also arranged teachers for them, so that they could study French.

Their arrival came, and they were so surprised to see Mona so elegant looking. They hugged and kissed constantly. They could not believe their eyes; she was so beautiful, and they couldn't stop looking at her. I had taken good care of her, having bought the most expensive dresses that existed on the market at that time. She looked like a queen. Hey, she *was* my queen, so I had to make her shine. Her mother started to cry with happiness. I told them how their future would look in Paris.

After a while, I left with her brothers and their families to give them the houses, and to introduce them to their personnel. My joy was immense when I saw their faces full of happiness, as if they had won the lottery. I had bought for them the most beautiful houses. The personnel were the best around, and I had prepared carriages for them to travel around the city.

Both of Mona's brothers started to bow, and their wives kissed my hand. I told Mona's sisters-in-law not to kiss the hand of anybody, especially men here in Paris. I specified that they are ladies, and here the men are kissing ladies' hands, not the other way around.

Her brothers had children, so I also had to provide toys and clothing to make them all comfortable. I told Mona that she should go shopping the next day to take care of clothing for her sisters-in-law and brothers.

Mona's mother lived with us. Her desire was to spend the rest of her life close to her sweet girl. She had missed Mona a lot over the past ten years. When Mona had left ten years ago, her mother had been very saddened, but there had been no other exit for Mona at that time.

The wedding day came quickly, and I made sure that all of her family were looking good and that they were happy and well treated in Paris.

During the marriage ceremony, everyone looked at Mona and admired her beauty. No one could take their eyes off her. Covered in of pearls and diamonds, she shone like a star in a night sky. I put all of the most expensive jewellery in the world on her, and she looked better than any storybook princess. Hey, you know me already—my love for her was bigger than all the jewellery from your planet. I made her shine from head to toe.

Our life together was magnificent. She gave me great gifts shortly after we got married: a boy and a girl. Both children resembled her, and they took from her tenderness and beauty. From me, they took my cleverness, because they were always joking around the house. In this life, she never wondered whether I was human or not. I do not think she knew what it meant to not be human— rather, I think she associated inhumanity with her father.

She always spoiled me, saying, "My lovely, rich angel." I liked the sound of those words coming out from her mouth. Although we lived a life full of great love and passion, we didn't accomplish the unconditional love she strove for. This time, she had imposed too many conditions again, and she hadn't let anything flow smoothly, but we lived happily ever after.

—Lucifer

7

Summer Vacation

My glass technology told me it was time to look for her again. I could see her resting on the beach. She looked sad and alone. As I was carefully observing her, I felt that something was wrong. I had to go to her now. She had a sinister plan to kill herself. I hoped that I could get to her in time, and so I left in a hurry. There was no time to prepare for the trip.

When I arrived on the beach I started looking for her, but I couldn't find her anywhere. I heard a noise—people were yelling, and then I saw two men carrying her in their arms. She appeared to have drowned.

Why did she do that? What had been happening in her life? I prayed to God I would get to her in time, as I rushed in her direction. Even I could not bring her back to life if it was too late or if her body was too damaged. The men had laid her on the sand and were trying to revive her, pressing on her heart and using a few resuscitation techniques at the same time. I arrived as fast as I could, and I told them that I was a doctor, so they let me revive her. After a few seconds, she opened her eyes and threw up water all over me.

While opening her eyes wide, she asked me, "Why, God?"

I said, "Why? Because you are gorgeous, and nature doesn't like to lose its beautiful women." She smiled, and at the same time she started to cry. I continued, "Dear, you are lucky today, because I am a doctor. Otherwise, you would be on the other side of the veil by now."

Her answer was, "But that is what I wanted to do."

I told the people around to leave, because she was okay now, and she needed fresh air.

I turned to her and said, "Welcome back to life!"

"I wanted to leave. There is nothing here for me to enjoy," she answered.

"It is wonderful here; there is a nice beach, great sun, gorgeous weather—why do you not enjoy all this? I want to introduce myself to you. My name is Aki, and I used to be a psychologist. Now, I am in a very successful business, and I gave up on my profession and left the medical field. I can see you are very sad, and that you want to die. You can trust me, because I can help you. Your first words when I revived you were, 'Why, God?' Well, I can tell you now that God sent me and that it was not your time to go."

She was surprised by what I had told her, and she looked at me with her big blue eyes, asking God and me for forgiveness of her suicide attempt. I held her in my arms until she felt better, and then I asked, "What is your problem, my dear? Why do you look so desperate and worried?"

"Okay, I will tell you my tragedy, but you have to promise me that you are not going to tell anybody."

"Okay. What bothers you so much and is worth your life?"

"Look, Aki, my name is Isabela, but my parents call me Ela. I am eighteen years old, and I am pregnant. That's the reason I want to die."

"I don't consider having a baby a reason to die so young," I replied. "What can you tell me about the child's father?"

"Oh, Alex is useless, and he ran away from me when he heard that I was pregnant."

"Okay, what is his age?" I asked

"He's the same age as me. We are colleagues, but Alex is not ready to be a daddy."

"You know, sweetheart, there are many ways to solve this problem. Losing your life is not the best choice."

"I didn't know what to do. I am over two months late, and my family doesn't know."

"Well, I understand your desperation, and I can help you to solve this problem. Do you want to keep the child?"

"Yes, I want to keep it, because I understand that getting rid of my child is a big sin."

"Taking two lives instead of one will be a bigger sin, don't you think so?"

"Oh, I didn't know that."

"It would still be considered killing yourself and the baby."

"I am so sorry. I never expected this to be a sin."

"Now, listen to this plan. I can help you with the baby, and, in the meantime, I will work with you to restore your happiness."

"Don't tell me that you want to marry me—or that you have somebody who would marry me—just because you are feeling sorry for me."

"Dear, I am sorry for you, but I do not want to get married to a girl for this reason, and I know of no one to marry you. I have a heart, and when I get married, I want my wife to fall in love with me. Otherwise, that person will not meet my criteria."

"Oh! You look so young, but you think like an old guy."

"Okay, sweetheart, listen here. This is how we can solve your problem with nobody knowing you are pregnant."

"Okay, I am listening with both my eyes and ears."

"First, after this vacation, you go home and say goodbye to your parents. Tell them you want to attend a school in another city, or maybe you are moving in with your boyfriend, or you found a job in another city. Tell your parents whatever you think is right. After you are done, I will wait for you in a nearby hotel, the closest one to your home. I will tell you the hotel's name and the room number so that you can find me easily."

"Okay, so where exactly are we going afterwards? I do not know you, and I don't know if this is the best choice for me."

"I promise to help you with the baby. Understand that you cannot give birth in a city where everyone knows you. What will you say to your family and friends, and how can you hide your pregnancy from them? Think again, sweetheart. You have to change the city first."

"Okay, you convinced me. What could be worse than what I just attempted?"

"You have this opportunity to change what is wrong in your life. Do you accept?"

"Okay, Aki. You are an angel, and I will come one day next week to your hotel, and I will take off with you into the big world. I will let you know the day and the time. Do you think it is a coincidence that you appeared in my life? I prayed so much to God to help me. Indeed, I appreciate that you were here to save me. You raised me from dead. I realized I was lifeless. How did you wake me up from death?"

"It's a doctor's job."

"I never heard of a doctor who could bring people back to life an hour after their deaths. I believe that God sent you, so I guess you are my guardian angel. Also, I saw you while I was dead, and you communicated with me. You instructed me to return to my body, because it was not my time to leave yet."

"You may consider me your guardian angel from your dream, but the truth is that this occurrence is just a coincidence. It happened to be on the beach when I heard screams and the cries of women for help. Because I am a doctor, I arrived to offer a helping hand as quickly as I could. I think you can consider today your lucky day, eh?"

"I suppose you are right, and I love you for what you are doing for me."

"Thank you. I am willing to jump in and help such a young woman at any time. I am just playing with you, of course. I would jump in for every person who requires help, because that is what doctors do."

&

When we returned from vacation, I waited for Ela to show up in my hotel the next day, in the afternoon. As promised, Ela appeared at my hotel, and, within hours, we left for Barcelona, where my home was. On the way back to my city, she felt awful, but after she vomited, she slept. The trip was long, and in her condition, it was better for her to relax and sleep.

When we reached my house, I helped her into one of the guestrooms, and I said, "You need to relax for a few hours, and I will order the dinner to be served later tonight. Is eight o'clock okay with you?"

She agreed, and then disappeared into her room.

At eight she appeared for dinner, smiling, and she looked

refreshed and relaxed. Ela resembled an angel, pure and innocent. While I stared at her, admiring her white dress with red polka dots, I decided to keep a cool attitude to make her feel more comfortable. I was feeling aroused from the liquor I'd drank before she entered the room.

I had to encourage her to fall in love with me again. Over supper, I asked many questions in order to understand what had happened in her life, and I explained my intentions to her. Looking at her with admiration I said, "Ela darling, you look like a bright star in the night sky. With your natural charm, you make me feel dizzy, but don't fear me, because I am harmless. I want to listen the story about you and your baby's father."

"Oh, Aki, I do not wish to remember this sad story, which could have ended in a tragic way. I was lucky you were there on the beach in that tragic moment."

"I want to make a plan to help you, and I need as much detail as possible."

"Yes, I know, but it is hard for me to remember and recount my life with him. Please, it's painful." Looking at me, she decided to confess, and she continued, "I will go over it and describe it to you. I have no other alternative. Right?"

"You need help, so go ahead, please. I won't share your story with anybody."

"We met in school, we were colleagues. His name is Alex. He followed me for a long time, and after a while, I allowed him to escort me home. It felt great, because somebody loved me, and he was courting me. My colleagues and friends had boyfriends, and I was the only one who didn't have a boyfriend. He had watched me since I was fifteen, but I hadn't paid him too much attention. In my imagination, I had created my dream boyfriend already." She paused for a minute, stared at me, and continued. "He is supposed to be older than me, because I love a sophisticated and romantic guy. Aged seventeen, I noticed that other boys didn't notice me, so I agreed to be Alex's girlfriend. We went out together many times, to the cinema and the parks, and we attended a few parties at our colleagues' houses.

"Five months ago, Alex invited me to his house, and he confessed how much he loved me. He made suggestions for our future, and we agreed to be friends until it would be a good time for us to get married. He suggested that we continue with school and get an education, as well as a profession, before we established a family. His analysis seemed mature enough, and I agreed with his ideas for our future. So, we raised our relationship up to another level. We kissed, and I had sex with him for the first time. I didn't wish to get pregnant, and I mentioned this to him, because I was not ready to have a baby. Apparently, he was more experienced than me in terms of sex, because he had been with other girls before me. So, he convinced me, and I let it happen. I guess I am too young, stupid, and naive."

"Did you fall in love with him?"

"Well, I do not think I loved him. I was thrilled because he was the only man following me around the school. I felt satisfied when he stated that he loved me and that he had serious intentions with me. His wish was to get married when we were ready to start a life together. I was delighted, because he loved me, and so I never took into consideration what I felt."

"And what were you feeling?"

"I felt guilty, but at the same time, I was honoured, because I had a handsome boyfriend. He had his way of touching my soul, and I ended up becoming his girlfriend. The girls from my school were staring at him, and this made me feel good about myself."

"So, you did not love him."

"I do not know, Aki, what it means to fall in love."

"It is when you lose your mind, and you do not know what you are doing. You cannot eat and sleep, and your heart beats faster when you are around him. You also think about him all the time, and your brain cannot think clearly."

"Honestly, I felt none of this."

"What happened? How did you get pregnant?"

"Aki, I do not know how it happened. Later, he told me that it was not his child, because he had had protected sex with me. I had had no one besides him. I liked none of the boys from my school, and I had to date him to be popular among my classmates."

"Now, here is my suggestion of how we should proceed. I will find a comfortable house for you. I do not want you to live with me; living alone would be the best way to preserve your reputation in this city. When the baby is born, I will put him or her in my name. Your name won't be in any of the reports as being the mother. You will change your name from Isabela to Gabriela. This is because I do not want your friend to find you, in case he remembers you and the baby. The harder to discover you it is, the better.

"I will arrange everything. You can relax, be calm, and enjoy the lifestyle you want so that you will have a nice healthy baby. If you ever meet Alex, and he inquires about the pregnancy and the baby, inform him that it was a false alarm. You have never been pregnant—just a few weeks late. Also, I want you to continue your education. Tell me what it is you want to achieve, and I will help you to fulfill your passions. Your baby will live with me after it's born. For those curious about the kid's mother, I will say that the kid's mom died in childbirth. I will adopt your baby, and you can come over when you want to see your kid. Also, I suggest breast-feeding the baby for a few months, if you do not mind. I'm an old-fashioned guy, and I know that is very healthy for the baby."

"Oh, my God, you are an angel sent by God. I cannot believe it. I am so lucky. What do I have to give you for this? Will I be your mistress?"

"Not even in your worst or graceful dreams. You will not be my sweetheart—you will be just a mother for your baby. Now, tell me, what do you choose for your education? Do you prefer to become a schoolteacher, a doctor, a lawyer? It can be whatever you want, because I will take care of everything."

"You will pay for everything, and you want nothing in return?"

"I do get something in exchange, however: an innocent infant. Because I am rich, I wish for my child's mom to be educated and rich. That is my intention. What do you think?"

"I cannot believe that something like this is possible. For my entire life, I've enjoyed piano and guitar, and so I would prefer to go to a school where I could study those instruments. My voice is beautiful, but I've never sung to anyone before."

"Okay, I will send teachers for you quickly, and I will find a nice house for you that's close to the baby."

"Aki, who are you? Why do you support me unconditionally?"

"I mentioned that I want a baby, and so this is a huge advantage for me. I registered to adopt a baby long time ago, but it was an extremely complicated process with a long waiting period. When I met you, I prayed to God that maybe you would give me your baby, so that I would not have to wait much longer."

"Excellent, but I do not understand. You are tall, handsome, athletic, rich, intelligent, mature, and well built. Why are you not married with your own children?"

"Okay, Ela, you're asking too many questions. My life belongs to me, as do my choices and decisions. It is my desire to help an innocent baby have a home and a rich dad. If I need more children, I will get married. Right now, I am too young to have a wife."

"How old are you?"

"Twenty-nine."

"At that age, you are already a doctor, a businessman, and you're rich. Also, you are too young to have a family, but you need a baby? I really do not understand you."

"Next month, I will be thirty years old. I'd love to have a baby, but not a wife—what is so hard to understand?"

Do you realize now how things progressed with Ela? I would move her into a house that was close to mine. I wished to see her daily. It was a start for me, and I didn't want any immature boy to come along and ruin her life. It had to be just me in her future, but she didn't know my intention. However, I would not agree to marry her if she never fell in love with me. We experienced a few lives together without being married because she preferred not to marry. I can tell you, it's a big difference; the love is not that deep. I loved the passion and the fire burning that burned our hearts and souls. We had that perfect love only when we got married.

Anyway, time ran on, and after a few weeks, I moved Ela into her house. Ela was delighted, and she could not believe everything was real. She was constantly admiring the house and the furniture. I presented her to the staff in the house. After a few days, she said that she loved the cook, because her food was delicious. I had made sure that I hired the best team to take care of her and to report to me what was going on in her house. I realized that what I was doing wasn't nice, but I had to watch her and make sure she was not dating the wrong boys. After all, she was going to be my wife, and I had arranged my plan according to my desires.

Ela was watching me from top to bottom, saying nothing, while I watched her, smiling full of love.

I said, "I am happy that you are pleased with the house and the cook. You can invite me for supper sometimes."

"I thought of that, but I didn't expect that you would accept my invitation."

"Why not?"

"I do not know, maybe because I didn't get a proper education in my parents' house, and I don't understand much. My parents were very busy working to make a living, and they didn't watch over me a lot."

"It will come to you, don't worry. I hired you teachers to help you finish your education. If your parents cannot afford to give you more of their time, I am here. It would be my pleasure to give you more attention, so that you can learn."

I could hardly keep myself from embracing her and kissing her from head to toe. I had to behave as a gentleman, however, in order to encourage her to fall in love with me. It was very hard for me to be an actor in every life she took. I knew who she was, and I wanted to marry her right away. Because of her desire to attain unconditional love, I had to wait for her to fall in love with me. Hiding our relationship from the other side of the veil was a very hard task for me.

However, time passed rapidly, and soon I had a daughter who was nearly a year old. She looked gorgeous, resembling her mom. Ela came daily to play with her daughter, and for a while she moved in with me to breastfeed the baby. I named the girl Sabrina after her mother's wish, and the nickname I chose was Ina. I preferred Ina, because this had been Ela's name in a past life—one where we were in love with each other, but fate had tragically separated us. Since then, her face and her name have stayed deeply embedded in my heart and soul.

৯৬

Years passed, and then Ela was twenty-two years old. She was a great opera singer, and she had the voice of an angel. Men swarmed around her like bees after honey. They invited Ela to dinners, dates, and parties. She attended a few parties, and she dated a few guys, but I was not sure where she stood in regards to her love life. While I took care of her from the shadows, I thought about how I could find out more. I wanted to know if she had any emotions for me. I didn't want to let other men grab her heart. They didn't know how to love, respect, and appreciate her—and besides, I was in love with her, so I had to arrange a path toward her heart.

One night after her opera show, I invited her to my house for dinner. I wanted to clarify what she was doing while dating other guys. *Where is her heart right now?* I wondered. For the past four years, my heart had been constantly with her. I did not receive a hint from her, or a sentiment other than friendship, affection, and respect. After hearing the invitation, her face was glowing, and she seemed delighted to have supper with me, but I didn't know if she considered this invitation a date or just a supper with an old friend. After the show, we headed to my house for dinner. When we arrived home, Ina rushed to me and yelled, "Daddy, daddy, my mommy is here."

Ina went up to Ela and embraced her mother with her small hands. Ela raised her up in her arms and started to smooch her with much longing. After a while, we lay on the couch and watched Ina play. We started speaking, and then Ina looked at Ela and turned to us. She took Ela's hand and placed it into my palm. Ela looked into my eyes and gave me a smile. She asked Ina about the purpose of this gesture. During this time, my hands were holding Ela's hands, and I could barely keep myself from shaking. Anytime I touched her, it felt as though electricity was going through my body.

Ina helped me again, saying to me, "You are my daddy." After pointing at Ela, she said, "You are my mommy." Looking at both of us, she wondered aloud, "Why do you live apart? Daddies and mommies live together."

We were lucky that Ina asked us this. Otherwise, our confession would have taken longer to manifest. I opened the discussion with a question. Ela usually asked questions, but this time I said to her, "Hey, Ela, forgive Ina—she doesn't know better."

I pulled my hands out from under her hands and looked into her eyes. I continued, "I see you have made a great success in music as an opera singer, and you've ignited the hearts of men. Men talk about you in the city—about your charm and talent—and many of them would love to marry you. Have you found a boyfriend? I think it is time for you to get married and have a family."

I think this was awfully hard on her. She became highly emotional and turned red. Then, she said, "Yeah, I think you are right. I've realized that it is time for me to have a husband and children. You've noticed how much I love kids, huh?" She stared long at me, and her eyes were drowned in tears.

I pretended not to notice, and I asked her, "Well, who is the lucky one?"

"I still do not know—I get hot flashes when I am with a man that I love. I dream about him for a long time, and then I am in love with him, but I do not know how to tell him."

Oh, no! I thought I had messed up badly this life. I thought I'd lost her already. *Am I too late?* I wondered. *She is in love, but who is the lucky guy?* I had to find out and put him on the run, because I could not endure seeing her with another man unless she was absolutely serious about him. If this is the case, I had already lost her on this timeline.

I asked, "Who is the lucky guy? Do I know him?"

"Yes, you know him very well!"

"Have you ever dated him?"

"Yes, but no too many times."

"Did he ask you to marry him?"

"Not yet!"

"He might be shy. Why haven't you told him that you love him?"

"Okay, I will."

This was harder for her than I had imagined. Her eyes were full of tears, and she could hardly refrain from crying.

"Hey, darling, you are wonderful, brilliant, and wealthy, and you are already a popular name in Spain. What makes you think that this guy would not ask you to be his spouse?"

"Well, Aki, it's time to go home. I don't feel well. I hope you will excuse me."

Then I said, "I am leaving tomorrow with Ina on vacation for two weeks. I would like you to come with us to spend more time with Ina, but I realize that you have contracts to honour during this time. So, we have to go on our own, because you are so busy with your profession."

Ela stared at Ina and me, wished us farewell, and then left.

She had broken my heart already, because she was in love with somebody else. At the very least, I had to find out who the lucky guy was. I send out a spy to observe her step by step while I was away with Ina.

The next day, I went with Ina to a nearby lake. We had a phenomenal time together. Whenever I watched Ina, I became lost. She resembled her mom from head to toe; they were like sisters. Anyway, the time passed slowly because I was away from Ela. *I must get used to the idea that she is in love with another man, and that she will marry soon,* I thought. I would prefer at least to continue being friends. If I got rid of her boyfriend, it could be a tragedy for her. Ela's heart was sensitive, and I did not wish her to repeat her crazy act of trying to kill herself.

Anyway, the time went by, and we returned home with many new toys and presents for Ela. I sent a message to Ela, telling her that we were back from vacation and that she was invited for supper, because we missed her. Because I had several hours until dinnertime, I asked my spy what he had discovered in the past two weeks. The guy giggled and said "Nothing." I asked him to describe what she had done for every hour of the past two weeks. He said that she had woken up around ten each morning, and after having breakfast, she would spend time in the garden by herself. A few times, she even ate her lunch in the garden. She seemed pensive and unhappy. He did not see a smile on her face other than when she was acting in the theatre. After the show, Ela was invited out for dinner several times by various men. She rejected them under the pretense she was tired.

"Well, what she was doing days and nights?"

"She was resting in the garden or on the terrace or she was playing sad music on the piano. Sara came over once, and they had tea together. She didn't stay for more than an hour. I guess she invited Ela somewhere, but Ela refused."

"Okay. Thank you for your services, and keep an eye on her. Tell me everything you see or notice. I have to go now, as I do not want to be late for dinner."

Dinnertime came, and Ela arrived. She was wearing a bright purple dress with silver accents. Her hat was silver with a big purple flower that highlighted her big, blue eyes. It was hard to watch her; she radiated beauty and delicacy that evening, and she smiled while approaching us. Ina ran to meet her mom, grabbed her hand, and then dragged her toward me. She kept repeating how we had presents for mommy.

Ela tried to look happy, but I could read on her face that she was very sad. Ina brought Ela closer, took my hand, and joined it with Ela's hand. I winked at Ina. Ela flushed, and she is uncomfortable with the scene Ina had produced. While holding her hands, I asked, "Hey, darling, how are you? Are we getting ready for the wedding? Have you solved the problem with your lover?"

She cried and declared that she had no boyfriend.

"Well, you were in love when I left for vacation. What happened?"

"I am in love."

"Okay. Who is the guy?"

"Somebody who ignores me all the time."

"Does he know about your feelings?"

"No!"

"Why haven't you informed him?"

"I am a woman—should I make him understand?"

"Well, sometimes it takes a woman to do that. What if he feels the same way about you, but he's just timid?"

"I do not think he is timid."

I guessed that the man she was talking about was me, but I was not completely sure. I had to find out.

I had waited for four years to kiss her, so I decided to try the kissing test and then look for her reaction. If I were the lucky one, she would kiss me back. If she rejected me, I would apologize.

I asked her, "Ela, what do you think? Do you want to walk through the garden with me after supper?"

Her face refreshed, and she replied with a loud "Yes." She turned it around, suggesting that we could benefit from the fresh air. It was a lovely evening, and walking in the garden would help us both.

We were occupied for a while with gifts, then with Ina's new toys, and then we had supper. After supper, Ina took the teddy bear her mom had brought and went to bed. Ina kissed us and said goodnight. Before we left her bedroom, she made me kiss her mom, because that is what daddies do. I had no choice, and I kissed Ela on the cheek. Ina smiled with enjoyment, and then went to sleep kissing her bear toy. After we had finished up with putting Ina to bed, we went out into the garden. We walked for a while, and after that we rested on a bench.

I asked, "Ela, out there are many guys who are courting you. Which one is your favourite?"

She said, "No one!"

"Well, you mentioned that you were in love with one of them."

She became very uncomfortable, and tears appeared in her eyes. I took her hand and kissed it gently, staring into her eyes. She radiated with joy. I embraced her with both my hands, and I kissed her passionately. She did not pull back, nor did she refuse me. *Hooray! I am the one!* I thought joyfully. *Will I be the winner again?* I must say, I had a lot of patience. Seeing and watching her every day, I worried about what she was doing with other men when she dated them. I thought several times that I might lose her.

Looking at her I ask, "Ela, am I the one you are expecting?"

She responded, "You are the one. I fell for you so hard, and you didn't even notice me."

"Honey, I waited for you for the past four years to fall in love with me. I thought I was clear when I mentioned how I wouldn't get married if the woman didn't love me with the same passion and intensity."

"Yes, I know what you told me. It is imprinted in my brain. I just never knew where you stood. Are you in love with me, or do you still consider me a good friend?"

"No, darling, I consider you my bride, and I fell in love with you when you were still pregnant. Do you remember? My love for you never died—it just became bigger and bigger."

"Oh, Aki! Why didn't you tell me this until today? You let me cry days and nights like a fool because I was loving a man who didn't notice me for the past four years."

"Frankly, I didn't know that I was the lucky one. I would never stand in the way of your happiness if you didn't choose me as your life partner. My love for you is more than you can imagine. It hurts me to see you with another man, but you are my treasure, the joy of my life. I would never do anything to make you unhappy and to force you to be mine."

"Therefore, even though you were in love with me, you were ready to sacrifice your life and watch me marry another guy? I do not understand. Why? If you are in love, why not show a sign?"

"As I said, you are the most precious gift I have from God, and I will do what you want to make you happy. You don't seem to understand this."

She kissed me passionately again. She knew how to get me, because she knew that I had waited a long time for this moment. Every time I wanted to say something, she covered my mouth with more kisses. I caught a moment between kisses to take a breath and ask her why she hadn't found another man, even though I had let her be free to choose.

She didn't answer right away. After a while, she said, "I keep comparing them with you. None of them have met my criteria."

Because it was getting late, we headed home in baby steps. I asked her if she wanted to go in the bedroom or living room for a refreshing drink. She said that she would leave that up to me; it should be my choice, because I was not ready for an intimate relationship. Now, she was playing with me, after she had kept me on pins and needles for four years. So, I took her in my arms and went straight to bed with her. She giggled with pleasure. I led her into bed, and I said that I would be back in seconds. When I came back, I could see that her face was curious, like a child's. I got on my knees and asked her to be my wife. She was stunned and speechless.

I said, "Before you change your mind and marry another man, I want to come and steal your heart forever, keeping it just for me. Do you wish to be mine forever? What do you say, my love angel?"

She seemed busy, and I realized I was speaking to myself. She admired the ring on her finger and kissed me at the same time. I asked again, "Do you want to be my wife? Because I am just getting older while staying here on my knees."

I heard a loud "Yes," and then she wrapped me up in kisses again.

She cried out loud, saying, "You've twice made me the happiest woman in the world, so a million times, yes, yes, yes!"

We agreed to plan the wedding quickly. I was thinking that if she became pregnant she would have qualms of conscience, because that would mean she would have a baby before marriage again. I knew she had done that before with her first child. It was tough to convince her otherwise.

&

While preparing the wedding, her boyfriend from school showed up at my house. Ela was not home when he rang the doorbell. I invited him in and inquired, "Who are you?"

"I am Isabela's ex-boyfriend, and my name is Alex."

"What do you want?"

"I need to see Isabela. I saw her in an opera advertisement, and I want to see my kid."

What a nerve this guy has, I thought. If she weren't such a big name in music, he never would have cared to inquire about her and the kid.

He had stunned me, and so I asked, "What child are you talking about? Isabela doesn't have any children."

"When we broke up four years ago, she was pregnant with my child."

"I do not know anything about this, young man. Maybe it would be better to wait and to talk to her about it in person. Right now, she is engaged with wedding preparations, and I do not know when she will be home. You can wait for her, or you may come another day when she's not so busy. By the way—why did you two separate, if I am not being too inquisitive?"

Alex replied, "She wanted to get married because she was pregnant and she didn't know what to do."

"What did you say when you found out about that?"

"I said that it was not my child, because we'd had protected sex."

"I understand; you didn't want to wed her because it wasn't your child. So why are you asking for your child now?"

"I don't think she had another guy, so now I am certain the kid was mine."

"With safe sex?"

"Yes, so I thought."

"What do you mean?"

"Look! I was inexperienced, young, and I had no money. Because of that, I had to reuse the condoms, and I found one broken."

"Oh! I understand now why you think you have a child. What can I tell you? I do not know if she has any children. I've known her for a few years, and I think that she would have told me that. At her home, I've never seen any child." I paused, then asked, "Alex, what are you doing for a living?"

"I am not doing well. I wanted to open my shop, but I didn't have enough money. So, I found a job in a store nearby."

"I understand. Oh, look, you are lucky, because Isabela is

coming now. I will leave you two alone."

Ela entered the house full of happiness and gave me a sweet kiss. While she was kissing me, her eyes stopped on Alex, and she asked him sharply, "What are you here for? What do you want?"

I left to give them some space, but Ela called for me to stay. She was talking sharply to Alex.

"Alex, answer the question, please."

"Okay, I came to see you and the kid."

"What kid?"

"Well, you were pregnant when we broke up four years ago."

"Alex, I came to tell you that the pregnancy had been a false alarm, but you were out with another girl. Then, you disgusted me too much. So, I left you, and you were able to get married to the right girl and pursue your dreams. Alex, I am glad I see you, but I hope that I won't see you again. When you thought that I was pregnant, you ran away from your responsibilities. I would be nobody today, and I wouldn't have been able to follow my dreams and put them into practice if I had been pregnant. I thank God it was a false alarm, and that I am what I am today: a very successful opera singer. What about you? Did you fulfill your dream of becoming a doctor or a lawyer? I do not remember exactly—what was your dream?"

"No, I work as a salesman in a store."

"Oh! I am sorry for you, and for your future. You are young, and so you can still change that and go back to school. I have to leave you now, because I am in a hurry, but please do not come back ever again—I will not be happy if you do. By the way, Aki is my husband. I forgot to introduce him. Sorry."

I took this opportunity to ask Alex where he lives.

"I am staying in a hotel until tomorrow, and after that, I will go back home," he replied.

"What hotel?"

"Santa Lucia."

"That is a nice hotel. Have a nice stay there."

So, Alex left unhappy. But why had he come? I didn't understand. Maybe he had hoped to marry Ela because he had made a kid with her and now she was rich. It was weird how, after four years, he suddenly wanted to be a father. Ela looked at me with pleasure, then she gave me a nice smile and a kiss and ran to Ina. She had bought something for Ina, and she wanted to surprise her.

The days went by, the wedding preparations were completed, and the wedding day arrived. Ela had invited half of the town to celebrate with us on this important day of her life. Ela's parents were jubilant over her achievements, and they wanted to move to our town to be close to us.

As the time passed, Ela became more charming and loving than ever. She was full of love and desire. From our ardent and passionate love, a girl was born. Ela knew that I wanted a boy, so we tried again, and we got another girl. Ela loved the girls very much, but she wanted a boy to make me happy. I was already happy and blessed with three girls—picky, fastidious, vicious, adorable, and all headed by their mother.

After a while, Ela found an astrologer and began calculating when she should try and get pregnant to have a boy. As a result, I became busy with the boy creation. Soon after, she got pregnant again and gave birth to our desired son. For her, having a son had become an obsession; she would have made twenty kids, giving birth until the boy came out. She loved to make me happy.

During this time, I was the happiest man on the planet, because

I was spending another life with my wonderful love partner. I was also content with my full house of noisy angels, all of whom filled our lives and hearts with happiness and gave meaning to our lives.

Regarding Alex, that evening I went to his hotel room. I gave him a tremendous sum of money to purchase his shop. I lent him the money without interest. I told him he could return the money when he had it. If I offered him the money as a gift, he would no doubt come back to ask for more. I made sure he wouldn't come back; the quantity I had given him was huge, just to be sure that he could never return it in his lifetime. This is an excellent way to get rid of the undesirable people from your life. Since then, I never heard of him, and he never came after Ela.

Ela's parents moved to our city and helped us with the children. This was great for me, because I could leave the house and go to my planet. I had to get the age changer working on me, so that I wouldn't have to answer Ela's questions about my roots.

Thus, our lives were full of happiness, joy, and four noisy kids. With regret, I can say that Ela didn't accomplish her goal of unconditional love again. She ran after this love concept every time she got a human body—which was not an easy task in a lower dimension. I was doing my best to help her, but it was hard for me, too. I wanted her to experience this concept with *me*, so I dedicated most of my life on planet Earth helping her to fill her contract.

—*Lucifer*

8

Twice in a Lifetime

Now I want to tell you another story of unfulfilled love, from my point of view. In this life, I was in love with Belinda, and she was in love with Nino, my rival in a few lifetimes. I came into her life, I disappeared, and then I reappeared again when the time was right for us to be together. Ada's name in that life was Belinda.

I remember when she met a man while visiting the pyramids with her parents and her sisters. The man she met there was Nino, her twin flame from the other side of the veil. He had taken a human body to help Belinda with her unconditional love experiment. This happened fifteen hundred years ago—Earth years. Therefore, a half-million years had passed since she had first taken a human body, and she still hadn't successfully completed the experiment. So, he showed up to help her.

I realized that I could not put up with a twin flame, so I disappeared. I was sorry to leave, but there was no way for me to get into her heart when her twin flame was around.

The moment she saw Nino at the pyramids, she fell in love

instantaneously. I am not sure what happened at the pyramids, but they lost each other. He searched the entire planet looking for her. As I re-examined the scene from my planet, I saw her losing her lover, so I thought I should take my chances with her again.

I appeared at her father's ballrooms and tried to win her heart, but she was so unhappy. Her heart was in another place. She didn't show up to many parties. I always waited until the end, but many times there was no trace of Belinda.

At the parties she attended, she was graceful, elegant, and delicate, but she also had a very cold behaviour. I couldn't take my eyes off her. I could read on her face how disturbed she was. Nevertheless, I took my chances again. I hadn't figured out how communicating with Nino for a few minutes had made her fall in love so deeply, to the point where she could never get out of it. I chatted and danced with her at every party and begged her for a date. She refused me every time. I didn't understand why, because she was single, anyway. One day, she informed me that she was in love, and she could not meet with me.

"In love with who?" I asked her.

She didn't answer. I knew Belinda's story very well, and I could have helped her find Nino, but I preferred to keep her for myself. So, I sat on the prowl, watching to see what she would do and how long she would wait for him. My love for her was very deep, but I respected her decision.

I visited her father many times for business purposes, and I tried again my luck.

"Dear Mohamed," I said, "I love your daughter, Belinda, and I am here to ask for her hand in marriage."

"My dear friend, I would be happy to give you Belinda in marriage, but you have to ask her first."

"You know that I am wealthy and that she would be the richest woman on the planet."

"I know that, Aki, and I also know that you are a diplomatic and intelligent man. You would be a perfect husband for her, and you have my blessings after she accepts you as her husband. See, I love Belinda very much, and I am not going to do anything to hurt her. If you are in love with her, just tell her, and maybe you'll get lucky. You know that she is wealthy too, and she will not get married if there is no love and passion from both parties."

We continued with a few business affairs, and afterwards I left feeling disappointed. Mohamed loved his daughters, and he made it clear: first the suitors had to get approval from the girls, and then from him. I did not know what to do, but I decided I would wait to see what happened.

This is the only timeline where I would marry her even if she didn't fall in love with me. Nino always managed to win her heart instantly, and I didn't want to let that happen. I've been jealous of him for eons. He has her in eternity. She should be with me while living on this planet, because she has had enough time to live with him.

Nino found her after one year, so I had to leave. I remembered that there would always be another life, so I could just wait for the next one.

As I watched her and Nino, a happy couple in love, I felt disappointed. I would have preferred to be in his place, but it wasn't meant to be. Here on my planet, I had the ability to watch her. I put my surveillance camera on her, and I programmed it to let me know if she was ever in trouble and needed help. She knew me, so it would be easy to reappear to help her.

Time passed rapidly, and after a few years, my machine rang the alarm, telling me that she was in distress and depressed. Looking at the record, I saw that Nino had had an accident and died. I came as quickly as I could. She was glad to see me, and she thanked me for coming.

After that, we started to spend lots of time together, but she never let me get closer to her heart. She was talking about her lover every time she saw me, and then she would begin to cry. I tried to calm her down every time she entered a great crisis over the loss of her lover. I struggled with her nervous system to bring it down to normal.

Many times, I told her, "My lovely Belinda, I don't want to lose you. I am hoping that one day you will marry me. We have been spending all our time together since the death of your lover. When you are ready, I am here to hold you."

I was talking to myself, because she didn't seem to see or hear me. Her mind was with Nino. He had left behind a profound wound in her heart and soul that wouldn't heal in that lifetime. I asked her to be my wife several times, and every time I was turned down she never heard my heart crying. She had never forgotten her lover. Even with all of my technologies, I couldn't help her to forget Nino. I showed up in her life daily, and sometimes I stayed close to her, living in one of her guestrooms. She would settle her head on my shoulder and start to cry, and my heart would cry too.

Honestly, I didn't know how to help her. She always wondered aloud to me, "Aki, why did God take my Nino? I do not understand. Please tell me why. God doesn't like me—I guess he hates me."

How could I answer such a question, especially because I knew that he had come to help her with her experiment of unconditional love? What was painful for me was that he had been able to help her with that experiment, and I was not. I wanted to be the one to help her achieve this concept of unconditional love.

I continued to be her valued and devoted friend, and I met with her daily until she died. I tried to be her boyfriend, but she refused me again and again. This was one of her lives where she rejected me before she united with her twin flame. Although she was not mine in body and soul, I was always beside her to protect her from her sorrow, suffering, heartache, and despair. I was glad that I could help her after she had experienced such a tragedy.

The loss of her lover marked her life forever, and she never let another lover enter her life. I was the only one she accepted in her life as a friend. I never said how much I loved her, and how much I wanted to be with her; I was afraid of losing her. I always thought that I could find a way to her heart, but I didn't. I imagined myself as her husband in that life, but somehow I couldn't tell her what was inside my heart. I got not a single sign that suggested she might want me as a husband. It was difficult, but I went through this with her many times.

So, twenty years after Nino's death, she was still mourning him. Her pain broke my heart, and I didn't know how to help her forget him. She dreamed of him every night, and she kept saying she'd seen him walking in the house. I do not think she wanted to forget or replace him in any way. She never left the house, and she received no one to visit besides her parents and sisters. I was the only other one accepted inside her house and her life. Her sisters tried to convince her to change her lifestyle, but she never accepted their recommendations. So, she stayed a widow with her heart burned until the end of her life. I occasionally healed the deep pain in her heart, but she always ended up in a depression. She knew about my healing powers, and I feel that's why she kept me beside her.

She never asked me, "Why are you single? Why you are not married? Why do you not have a woman in your life?" I don't think she understood that *she* was the only woman for me in that lifetime. In her situation, she never understood how much I loved her, and how much I desired her. Also, she didn't see or feel the sorrow and the pain in my soul. As always, she considered me as one of her employees, or maybe a devoted friend.

After so many years, I guessed I wasn't bright enough. I knew I should try to make her happy, but I didn't know how. I tried all the methods I knew, but they didn't work.

Because of this tragedy, she hated herself, Nino, and God. She never understood that there was a reason why things happened the way they did. Also, she didn't believe in life after death, nor God. She still prayed to God because she had grown up with that tradition, but deep down in her heart, God didn't exist. I calmed her down by telling her that there is life after death, and that she would be there one day with her lover. This gave her a little hope, but she didn't trust me completely.

She didn't live too long, because the pain took her life early. I sensed that she was not feeling well, but she said nothing about it. Looking at her, I understood that she wanted to go, and that she didn't need healing or other treatments.

Maybe if we had married and had children she would have passed through that life more easily, but she never wanted another relationship. During that life, her grief was more than she could handle. I was glad that she let me stay beside her, so that I could take a little bit of the burden that she carried on her shoulders.

Thus, even if she didn't want me, I took care of her. I never left her alone, and I stayed with her all the time. I never abandoned her, even in those lives where she was not in love with me. My love for her is like a fire that never dies. I harboured her in my heart forever, even though she had chosen another entity for her eternity, her twin flame.

ॐ

After the death, you all lived only with me in the heaven that I create for you. At that point in my life, I was very greedy, and I didn't want Belinda to meet Nino on the other side of the veil. My passion for her was so deep, and I didn't want to share her with anyone. Now, it is different; I am *all love,* and we lived together as *one.*

On the other side of the veil, Nino knew about the contracts on Earth, but he didn't know where to locate Belinda in her spirit form. This worked perfectly in my favour. Am I to be condemned for this? After all, she had accepted and conformed with the contract. Me? I picked up just a few advantages out of it. She was mine, anyway.

After my departure back home, I spent thirty earthly years in the light chamber. When I got out from the light chamber, the first thing that came to my mind was: *Where is she? What is she doing?*

When I found her again, I used my entire collection of tools to make her contact me, and there we were, together again and residing in different dimensions.

—*Lucifer*

9

Alien Life

Now I want to tell you about a very unusual life I shared with Ada. I enjoyed that life very much, and I was delighted by how easily she seemed to accept the truth about me. She was not afraid of who I was, but even now, I am not sure if she took me seriously.

She was born in Brazil this time, and her name was Sabrina. She had many reincarnations in Brazil. I believe she liked this country very much. I looked in my agenda, and I saw that she was around the age of maturity. There I was again, trying my luck and helping my dear friend with the project of unconditional love.

Once I was in Brazil, I followed her after school hours. I tried to talk to her, but she refused me every time. I didn't give up on her so easily, so I followed her on daily basis until she accepted a date.

One day on her way home after school, she was surrounded by a few individuals older than her, and they were bothering her. First, they took her school backpack and threw it, and then they pulled her skirt high to look at her feet. They laughed and joked around. She snapped and hit one of them with a plank she found on the road. She was furious and demanded to know who was next. She started yelling for help. I rushed to get there quickly.

When I arrived, she was shaking, and she was very nervous. I think she was scared that things would take a violent turn. When I approached her, the guys ran away, and she remembered me right away. She was lucky that I hadn't given up on her so easily; I was following her because I needed to talk to her. She apologized for not giving me attention over the past few days.

I walked her home, and then I suggested a date for the following evening. She was confused, but she accepted my invitation. She mentioned right away that she only wanted to go with me to public places, because she was feeling nervous after the confrontation. I told her that I was mature and that I held no similarities with those guys who had assaulted her on the street.

She asked, "How old are you?"

"Thirty-one."

"How do I know you are not like them? I just met you, and I know nothing about you."

"I am alone, I am mature, and I respect women. Why should I profit off you?"

"Okay, but I am only eighteen. Don't you think that's a big age difference between us?"

"I say that we see each other a few times, and if you believe you are too young, I'll wait for you to grow up."

She laughed and said, "Okay, you convinced me. I'll meet you tomorrow at six in the afternoon. Do you want to see a movie?"

"We will have a supper together, and after that, we can see a movie or a show, whatever you choose."

"Okay, I'll see you tomorrow."

She studied me from head to toe, smiled happily, and then replied, "Are you truly thirty-one years old? You do not look that old."

"I was joking; I am only twenty-six years old. I completed my schooling this year."

"What are you doing for a living? And what school did you attend, if I'm not being too inquisitive?"

"Law school, but I would prefer to start a business. I haven't determined yet what business. I am not Brazilian; I live in the USA, and I am here for a short vacation. Also, I wish to devote this vacation getting to know you better. What do you think?"

"You do not wish to meet other girls?"

"No, I would prefer not to. You have in you something that delights me in a magical way. Because of that, I would prefer to spend my time only with you, to discover why I am so attracted to you."

"Okay, I understand. I already noticed something too, because you look familiar—I think I know you from somewhere."

"It's impossible, because this is my first visit to Brazil. My friends have visited Brazil many times, but I haven't. They told me that in Brazil there are charming and brilliant girls. So, I showed up to find a girl, and if we fall in love, I am ready for marriage. I have been searching for a long time to discover the perfect girl for me. But now, I have a feeling that I found my dream girl."

"Hey, you're making my heart beat so fast that I feel baffled. I have not completed school yet. In fall, I will go to university."

"What will you study?"

"I wish to become an English teacher. I love mathematics too, but I prefer foreign languages."

"That is nice. Maybe you will also accept a partner in your life."

"Yes, I think that our relationship could be amazing, and I am feeling good. I must leave you now, and I will see you tomorrow afternoon at six."

The next day, as promised, I presented myself at her door. Her mother invited me inside to wait until Sabrina was ready. She served us tea, and we chatted about Sabrina's future intentions. Her mom sounded like a smart and educated woman. She said she was a physician, and that she wished for Sabrina to become a doctor, as well. But Sabrina didn't want to become a doctor. For her mother, Sabrina's individual wishes were more important than continuing the family tradition. Sabrina's dad was a surgeon, and he was working at the hospital.

Soon, Sabrina appeared, glowing like a star with a smile on her face.

"Hello, sorry for the wait," she said. "I am ready to go now."

I said goodbye to her mother, and I took off with Sabrina.

I had made a reservation for supper at a famous restaurant in the city. On our way to the restaurant, she laughed and said, "I do not know your name, and you don't know my name yet. Ha, ha! How mysterious is that?" She continued laughing.

"Huh! I know from your mom that your name is Sabrina. My name is Aki. Nice to meet you, darling."

"What kind of name is 'Aki'? Your name is unusual."

"It is a nickname, from Anunnaki."

"Okay, it's not relevant! So, where are we going?"

"To a restaurant near your home. Sabrina, please tell me, what are your passions in life? How do you want your boyfriend or husband to be? Do you have any preferences?"

"Of course I have preferences, but I haven't searched for the dream prince yet, because I am busy with my schooling. Also, my big dream in life is to find out more regarding aliens and UFOs."

"How do you expect your dream prince to be? What qualities must he possess?"

"He must be intelligent, rich, spontaneous, open minded, knowledgeable, good looking, a gentleman, and, most importantly, we must both fall in love with one another. If I do not perceive the feeling of love, I will not get married. I would prefer him to be easygoing, and to love me passionately. Do you know someone who matches those qualities?"

"Yes, me! And, as a bonus, I am romantic, tender, and eccentric."

"Oh! I love that in a man. Are you sure this is all true, or are you lying to me?"

"My dear, I indeed have these qualities, and more. For example, I am very different from the men you know."

"You know, I'm starting to like you. What makes you believe that you are distinct from other men?"

"I'll let you guess."

Jumping from one thing to another, we arrived at the restaurant. It was noisy, because there was live music playing, and so we couldn't communicate too much. I noticed that she kept peeking sideways at me. I guess I made her curious.

After dinner, we danced, and then we left the restaurant. It was too late to go to a movie or a show, so I invited her for a short walk in the nearby park.

I asked, "How have you felt this evening, my lady?"

"Honestly, I liked your company, and I hope to see you again. There is something in you that intrigues me, stirs me, delights me, and disturbs me at the same time. Also, it was wonderfully satisfying being around you and communicating with you. You know that I sense that I've known you for a long time, and this puzzles me, because you mentioned it's impossible that we ever met."

"I followed you on the street three times this week, because I saw you when you left the school. I was in the park across the street, sitting on a bench, admiring the landscape. When I looked at you, my heart jumped, because you looked exactly like the girl of my dreams. I tried communicating with you, but you refused my company. After that, I waited each day in front of the school, following you and struggling to talk to you. Not a chance—you ignored me each time, but I do not give up on my dreams so easily. When I saw a few boys ambush you on the street, I was behind you, watching the scene. I didn't know if they were your friends or colleagues. When I saw how they treated you, I hurried to help you. I assume that's why you recognize me from someplace."

"I thank fate that you were there, otherwise I don't know how I would have escaped from last night's incident. You were my big hero. And now, dear Aki, what is your opinion of our date?"

"Frankly, I like you very much, and I wish to see you every day—if it's possible—until my departure. I want to see if there's a spark of love between us."

"I am interested in this relationship too, because you fill my heart with pleasure when I speak with you. I also hope I can see you again. It would be a pleasure for me to meet you on a daily basis until your departure. You are an attractive man, properly educated, super bright, and I am attracted to you very much."

"Then I will walk you home now, because it is getting late, and I promised your mom that I would bring you home early. I will come tomorrow at three to take you out. We may have time for a movie or a show, and then we can have dinner together. What do you say?"

"Yeah! Sounds wonderful! See you tomorrow!"

કે

The next day, I picked her up from home, just as we had arranged. We went to watch a film that Sabrina had wanted to see for a long time. After the film, we went to a nearby restaurant for supper. Our night was full of magic, wonders, and the desire to understand and discover more about each other.

Time passed rapidly, and after two weeks, I dared to share a kiss with her as walked toward her home. It had been a pleasure for me to wait, and I wanted to see her reaction. I was impressed, because she expected this, and she kissed me back strongly.

I had to leave her because it was getting late, and on my way home, I wondered if there had been a spark of love. Was it too early for her to fall in love? I was searching for that spark to make me feel better. Otherwise, I would have to use my tools to test her. While I was watching her, I saw a strong girl—confident, with a high self-esteem—who treated me like her best friend. I didn't know what was in her heart. During our dates, I had noticed that she never kissed me first, but she always responded passionately to my kisses.

I thought there might be something in her heart for me. I am a simple guy, and I never used more than two procedures with women: the kissing test, and the test of leaving for a short period. I guess it was time to leave the country to find out more.

Since my departure time was coming quickly, I told her that I had to leave soon. I saw she was sad, and I mentioned that I would be back in a month. I would actually come back to Brazil within two weeks, because I didn't want to lose her. Living away from her was not acceptable for me, in case she was able to find another guy. Therefore, I had to return quickly. In the meantime, I would ask my guys to watch her every move. When I would get to the USA, I would figure out more.

The day arrived for me to leave, so I kissed her goodbye. She kissed me back, and she said that she would wait for me. She didn't seem too sure that I would be back, so she became suddenly cold.

I left Brazil the next morning. My heart and my mind were always with her. I couldn't find my place. Nothing felt good, and I was stressed over how to proceed. I was thinking, how will I resist staying away from her so long? My decision was to return to Brazil within two weeks, but I had to go back in eight days with a plan. I missed her so much that I couldn't sleep and eat much while I was away from her. I had my favourite drinks, and I dreamt of her.

❧

After I arrived back in Brazil, I went straight to her house. I knocked on the door, and she opened it wide, jumping into my arms and kissing me. It was easy to see how much she enjoyed my arrival. I informed her that I had a surprise for her.

"My dear, I have arranged for you to continue your education in the USA."

She looked delighted and said, "Oh, this is wonderful! But, we have to talk with my parents. It will probably be too expensive, and I do not know if they can afford to pay for my school in the USA."

"Well, my dear, it will not cost much. I have arranged things with a few businesses to pay for your school. They have scholarship programs, and I put you on their lists. I can help with sheltering you during your school years at my aunt's house. She is rich, and she has a few servants. You will love her—she is nice and has a good heart. I think you two would get along together."

"Okay, that sounds great! I think you should come tonight to have supper with my family. Explain to them what you told me."

"This is wonderful! What time?"

"Six will be okay; they will be home by then."

"Good, I will see you at six tonight." I gave her a kiss, and I left.

❧

I was getting ready to inform her parents that it was better to study English in the USA than Brazil. I hoped my plan would work and that I could convince them of this opportunity. I realized it would be tough to convince them, because she was their only child, but I would put my charm and my strategies to work.

At six, I went to Sabrina's house. She had already informed her parents of the opportunity that had arisen. I described all of the details, emphasizing that it was going to be extremely cheap for them, with school and her books paid for and her shelter figured out. I would take care of her transportation while she lived in the USA, and the only money she'd need would be pocket money for things such as movies. As I watched, they looked concerned, and then surprised. They asked for a few minutes to talk to each other alone.

After a brief period, they returned and said, "I think this plan is wonderful for Sabrina. It is better for her to learn English in the US, because she has the opportunity to speak English every day. We have enough money invested to pay for her expenses in America. You mentioned that you have arranged free education and a place for her to live. This sounds wonderful! Our only wish is to go with her to the USA when school starts. I think you understand that we would want to be comfortable and to have peace of mind while she lives in the USA."

"I am glad to hear that. It will be no problem for me to accommodate you in my house while in the USA. Also, feel free to come anytime during school time to see Sabrina. It would be a pleasure for me to be your host any time you come to my country."

Looking at Sabrina, I saw she was radiating joy. She said, "Mommy I want to say something. I am delighted to live in the USA, but I also need to tell you that Aki is my boyfriend, and I love him. There may come an opportunity to marry him and stay in the USA—but only if he is in love with me. I won't marry soon, but if the time comes, I will keep you posted."

I stared at her. She seemed to be provoking me to say something about our friendship and possible marriage. Now, what do you think about that? What a smart girl. Who knew that she would shift our relationship around so soon? As I watched her, I wondered why she never wanted to kiss me first, but she was speaking of marriage before me. Women are extremely complicated as you can see, and it's so hard to figure them out.

Because everyone was staring at me, I said to her parents, "I met your daughter over a month ago, and I fell in love with her in the first week of knowing her. I love Sabrina very much, and I do not want to force her to do anything. I am waiting for her to fall in love with me. Then, we will decide together what we want to do. For me, it is a pleasure to hear that she is already in love with me. Of course I want to marry her, but I believe it would be better to be friends for longer before marriage."

Her parents were delighted with the situation, and they began to congratulate us both. Her dad said that if we decided to get married, we had his blessings.

It was late, and I was preparing for my departure when Sabrina pulled me by the hand and led me into an adjoining room to chat.

"I guess everything worked out perfectly," she exclaimed enthusiastically. "I did not foresee everything going so smoothly."

Holding my hand, she continued, "I never told you, but I meant every word I said. I am certainly in love with you, but I wouldn't consider being your wife or your girlfriend if you are not in love with me. I thought I should mention that. My intention is to live a dreamy love story together. I see that you are a romantic man, and I admire that in you. As I've watched you for the past month, everything you say and do delights me. When I go to the USA with you, I will be ready for a powerful love story with my boy-friend. What do you say? You keep staring at me and smiling. Do you feel the same, or are you just pretending? I would be extremely disappointed if you just pretended to love me."

"Well my dear, I fell in love with you in the first week I saw you, as I explained to your parents. I meant every word I said. I am happy to be the one to try and achieve your dream love. We have known each other for over a month, and you have already stolen my heart. So, my love, I will be fortunate to have you in my country. Having you there will be much smoother for the both of us in taking this relationship to the next level. I am delighted that your parents will come with us to the USA. I never told you, but I am a wealthy man, and I predict that your parents will be delighted to live with me while in my country. It's a brilliant decision, and if I become a parent, I will do the same for my daughter."

I had to leave because it was late, and I kissed her hand while staring at her. She held my head between her palms and kissed me with passion. Hooray! What had happened? She had never initi-ated a kiss until now.

I couldn't wait until August to get her in the US. I arranged with her parents to come out one month prior to the start of school. That way, we could go on a short vacation together, and we could visit a few interesting places. They agreed.

Finally, the long-awaited day arrived, and we all went together to the US. I sheltered them in my house until I had resolved every-thing. My guys found a school for Sabrina, and I spoke with my friend Betty about housing Sabrina while she was in school. When I visited Betty, I explained to her that she had to act as though she was my aunt. She understood.

I went to school to register Sabrina and pay her tuition fee, and while I was there I donated extra money to help them improve their school system. They were fortunate to have Sabrina as their student, as well as a wealthy sponsor for their school.

After the preparation was done, I moved Sabrina to Betty's house. Her parents agreed to live with me until their departure. We got along well together, and it was a pleasure for me to have them in my house. Because of this, Sabrina would come over ten times per day to see her parents. This situation was in my advantage, as you can see.

After all the arrangements with the school had been made, I took Sabrina and her parents for a short vacation around the US, and we visited a few cities, as well as a few other remarkable places. Her parents were delighted by the beauty of nature, and they treated me with love as their future son-in-law. The vacation went by quickly, and we returned to my city because school was starting in a few days.

Everything went well. Sabrina started the school, and her parents beamed with joy. I had to arrange for them to get back home.

Time went on, and then we were alone. I wanted to tell Sabrina the truth about me. I was curious about how she would take it. I was not in a hurry, but I wished to take our relationship to the next level. She was open minded, and she had a great passion for aliens. She read all the books about aliens and UFOs that she could find, and she was excited by them. To me, it looked like she was in love with them, not me.

Sabrina told me excitedly—and with considerable detail— about what she knew about aliens. This made me feel comfortable in declaring the truth about me. If she wouldn't understand or accept me as an alien, I did not know what I would tell her. I didn't want to lose her, so I had to be careful and have a proper backup plan; I didn't think this was necessary, but you never knew, with her. She had her moods and was somewhat unpredictable. So, if she liked or wanted something today, she might not choose it tomorrow.

Next day, we had a date. She was excited over the dream she had had last night, and she insisted on informing me of all the details. I listened attentively, because I had given her the dream. She said, "I dreamed how a UFO came and grabbed me, and I flew around, and I went to another planet. I loved it. But you know what? The person on the UFO was you. I was so fortunate to have my dream prince coming with me to another planet. What do you think this dream means? Could it be because you moved me to your country and you helped me with school and the rest? I don't understand the true meaning of the dream, but I loved it, and I didn't want to wake up."

I took advantage of the situation. "Well, Ina," I said, using the name I had heard her mother calling her, "the absolute truth is that the dream was real. I am an alien, and my original house is on another planet, not here."

I looked at her, trying to detect her feelings, just in case I had to switch my words around and convince her that it had been a joke.

At first, she looked surprised and puzzled, then she laughed and said, "Really, you are not human?"

"No, I am not."

"I thought so—there is something in you that sets you apart from everyone else. Can you tell me if you can get me to your world?"

While I stared at her, she began to make arrangements for the future, embracing me excitedly the entire time. I pulled out the ring from my pocket, and I asked, "Sabrina, do you want to be my wife?"

She looked shocked and delighted, and she started to kiss me, and then she yelled "Yes!"

"I have a question. If I wasn't an alien, would you still marry me?"

"Yes! Yes! Yes! You forgot that I fell in love with you before you informed me that you are an alien. Now that I know who you are, I would prefer to go with you wherever you choose. You have my heart eternally."

What do you think of this surprise? Who could have known that she was so eager about aliens and that she preferred one as her man?

I said, "What do you think, can we go to my planet before our marriage? I want you to be comfortable with my home. But if you do not like it, you can change your mind."

"You have to understand one thing: I agreed to be your companion whether you were human or not, and to live on this globe or elsewhere. Darling, you look more human than other humans I know. I fell in love with you before I knew the truth, and my feelings for you didn't change upon hearing your story. You know what? I am fortunate, because I have both you and the alien you."

She began to passionately kiss me again, while she nagged me about when we could go to my planet. She asked me to explain more about myself and my life outside Earth.

I said, "Do you wish to know who I am?"

"Of course. I want to know because it is becoming progressively more exciting."

"Are you confident that you won't get scared?"

"You don't intimidate me; you make me laugh. No matter who you are or what you do, you are mine, and I would not give you to anyone. You are my expected angel. So, what do you say, my sweet angel? Do you realize that angels are not humans?"

"What if I am not a wonderful angel, and I am an evil one—the one you fear in your doctrines?"

"You mean Satan."

"Yes, the evil guy from your Bible."

"This is becoming more exciting. Are you Satan?"

"Yes!"

"I cannot believe that I am so lucky! I'm with the bad aliens' leader."

"Aliens are not all bad individuals. Did you know that?"

"Yes, I realize that, but when we speak about aliens, we only think about the evil ones."

"You know now who I am. Are you still going to marry me?"

"Are you kidding me? If you are Satan, and you are the head of the evil aliens, and the one who intimidates us, I will declare again: yes! I will marry you, because I choose to be the wife of the smartest man in the universe."

What can I say? She touched my heart and soul with her replies. She knew who I was, and she still wanted to wed me. Did you foresee that? Did you expect this girl to be so open minded and to consider Satan the smartest man in the universe? Now, I had to ask her another question. "My dear sweet lady, do you want to be Satan's bride?"

"Are you asking me to be your wife a second time? I already informed you before."

I took her in my arms and kissed her with passion and satisfaction. She checked my head to see if I had horns and then laughed loudly and kissed me back. I didn't think I needed an answer to my question, because we had our first hot night together, and it was full of passion, fervor, and fire. A union through marriage was no longer needed, because our hearts wanted something deeper.

I wasn't sure if I was the smartest man in the universe, but I was certainly the happiest and the luckiest one.

Now, after all my time with her various reincarnations on planet Earth, she was the only one woman who ever lived with me on my planet. I could never influence my other wives to leave planet Earth and live with me in my kingdom.

Now, let's get back to our story. Since her parents had left the country, we were able to spend more time together, and she was pressuring me to go to my planet. Because she didn't want to stay in Betty's house, she moved in with me. I watched her with immense pleasure and appreciation, because she put passion into everything she undertook.

She nagged me again, asking, "Aki, how long is the trip to your planet?"

"If we're using Earth time, it should be under one hour—I believe around forty minutes."

"That's fantastic, when are we leaving?"

"When you choose. Talk to your school, and let me know when you are able to go."

"Okay, can we go tomorrow?"

"Yes, sure, we can go tomorrow. I miss my home."

"Should I prepare any luggage?"

"We do not have to carry anything. I have everything we need."

"Should I bring clothing with me?"

"No need for that, we have technology that will produce clothing for us in less than five minutes."

"Well, that's easy—I don't have to bring anything with me."

"Well, you have to bring something."

"What's that?"

"Don't neglect to take Satan with you. By the way, I would prefer it if you called me Aki or Lucifer. I like these names better."

"Okay, my dear Lucifer. Do you want to come with me?" While she talked, she was hanging from my neck and kissing me lovingly—the way that pleased me.

The next day, we left for my planet. I could see happiness and joy on her face. She kept asking questions, such as, "Can we inhale the air on your planet, or does it require oxygen tubes?"

"There is no need for oxygen cylinders. Our air is similar to the air here—it's just fresher and not polluted."

"Okay, and do you have water?"

"We have water, and it is tastier than the water on Earth. Drinking this water, we do not age."

"You mean if we stay on your world, we no longer grow old?"

"Well, we do age, but it takes longer than on planet Earth. A day on my planet is one year on your planet."

"I guess we are moving there."

"Wait to see if you like it, and afterwards you can decide."

"I've decided now—we are moving to your planet."

"What if you dislike it?"

"If I have you with me, I will love it."

"Okay, sweetheart, it's whatever you choose, because what I wish is not important."

I smiled at her. She filled my heart with unexplained magic and wonder, as well as enjoyment and affection.

"You are the most powerful man in the universe, and you are mine, and I will not share you with anybody. Now, please tell me why you came to Brazil? On your planet, do you not have girls?"

"Yes, we have many girls, but none of them is as remarkable and bright as you. I have the ambition to marry a girl different from those on my planet. So, I landed on planet Earth to choose one. When I saw you, I fell in love instantly. After that, I asked myself, 'What will she do when she finds out that I am not human?'"

"As I've said, you seemed more human than the real humans I've met."

While we chatted, we arrived at my planet. I observed her to see how she was doing. When she got out of the UFO, she breathed in deeply to see if there was enough oxygen for her in the air. Then she searched around and admired the nature. Our nature was the same as on Earth, with a few variations, because in my world, we preserved the original wilderness. After she had turned around three hundred sixty degrees, she grabbed me with her arms and kissed me excitedly. I guess she liked it.

Our transportation arrived to get us to my house. She was astonished; she was flying in a car that operated at an incredible speed. We did not have private transportation here. We wandered around by flying or by using an electromagnetic car.

I ate very little on my planet, and instead I drank plenty of water. We didn't have kitchens. A few of us picked up food from machines on the streets, and in each house, we had a technology that prepared food when we wished.

In addition, our society was organized differently than planet Earth's, because it didn't have so many hierarchies. We had responsibilities, but we worked fewer hours than you did. Our society did not need money or other currencies like the ones you have on planet Earth. Our duties were done from our homes, and the heavy-duty jobs were done by robots.

Looking at Sabrina, I guessed everything would go smoothly. She was so in love with me, and she didn't care much about the details around her or even who I was. This came as a surprise for me, because I hadn't expected that she would be so comfortable with me after knowing the truth.

She gave up on her courses at the university. I downloaded the English language into her mind, and then she could speak like an

English-born citizen.

Sabrina preferred to live in my world. In the beginning, she often visited Earth to see her parents. Every time we went back to Earth, she was passing through an unhappy period, feeling homesick. I advised her to bring her parents to my planet. She said that she didn't think they would come. Besides, it was better for them to not know who I was and where I lived. That would embarrass them.

In one of our visits to planet Earth, we went to Brazil and had a big wedding. Sabrina's parents were very happy for us. They understood that we were very much in love after a year of knowing each other. We visited her parents annually. After they died, Sabrina never went back to planet Earth.

Because she was a dynamic woman, I created for her a department to work on her ingenious ideas. She was particularly good at solving problems, and she was constantly coming up with solutions to upgrade the technology we had. Sabrina had excellent intentions to invent new technologies, and she had a brilliant mind for creating impossible and fantastic things. She didn't know how to produce them, but she would bring me the plan, and I would analyze it and give it to my people for implementation.

I can say that many of the advanced technologies of my world were her mental creations. She created the design and then drew them out. Don't get me wrong—she had no knowledge of how to produce them, but she had a rich vision of how technology should be, in order to improve our lives.

❧

The time passed, and I asked her if we could have a baby from our ardent love. She responded that she would think about it. I wanted a baby, but I would have to wait until she was ready. I was lucky because she didn't age, otherwise we would have had to give up on kids.

She was on my planet for a month, which equals thirty years on your planet. During this time, her parents died. She was busy visiting various places on my planet.

After a while, she nagged me to visit other planets. She demanded to see their technologies and ways of life.

To make the story short, I went with her to several planets where it was accessible for me to go, but I did not have access to every planet. The planets around function on light technologies, and they are imperceptible to us. Those technologies are not functioning on my planet because of the difference in frequency. My planet vibrates on a lower frequency level than other planets. For me it was easy; I could see them and interact with them, but for her they were invisible. I explained to her about their way of life and their technologies, so that maybe she could come up with an idea or two.

I had to hide from her that the entire universe was inhabited by advanced civilizations, otherwise she would have wished to visit all of them. I could not enter most of the planets and stars, so I explained to her they were not occupied, because they couldn't sustain life. I mentioned that the atmosphere on those planets differs from ours, and she gave up on her experiments.

When she had nothing to do, she became bored, and this was a proper time for me to bring up my wish of having children. It was difficult to convince her to have that first baby, but after that, it was simple. She saw how the baby filled up her life and heart with joy and satisfaction, and she was not bored anymore. Because of this, she wanted more kids. I was delighted with this turn of events, and I became very busy. In this life, she gave me eleven kids. I do not think she knew how many she had. When a kid grew up to be three years old, she wanted another one. She adored babies.

We lived together for one hundred fifty years, which equalled many more years on planet Earth. Maybe today we would still be together, but she lost her body in an accident. She created a unique technology, and she wanted to be around for its testing.

A powerful explosion took place, which took her life. I couldn't save her, as her body was extremely burned and damaged. I put her on our healing machines, but it wasn't possible to recover her. It never occurred to me to make a copy, or clone, of her while she was still with me.

As you can see, our story was extraordinary, but it ended tragically. Her entire family missed her, and our friends from my world longed for her spiritual warmth, her inner beauty, and her passion for life. For me, it was a big heartbreak, but I knew I could have her in the next life.

—*Lucifer*

10

The End of the Journey

Life on Earth is an extension of life in the spirit world, and by now you should understand a little about your own beautiful journey on planet Earth. Here in the spirit realm, we considered all of you heroes, as you are the most courageous and brave souls, who offered voluntarily to experience living in a lower frequency realm. You are evolving now on many other frequencies and different lifelines.

As per your new prophets, you are multidimensional spirits who are one with God. There is no difference between you and God, and there is no difference between you and other humans, or even non-humans. The differences appeared when you arranged for yourself to be detached from the source.

I helped you to become separated. When you started the journey, you knew that it would be extremely painful to live in survival mode, temporarily cut off from the source. Decreasing your energy to reach a lower frequency level was the only way you could experience third-dimension frequency.

Before you volunteered for this experiment, we knew together that it was hard to live in a lower frequency field. When you live in higher frequency, such as *love*, you cannot experience emotions of a lower frequency, such as *fear*. You are God's masters, who have experienced all the frequencies of the universes. When you come back home, you will have lots of experiences to share with your brothers and sisters. They will be delighted to listen to your stories, because they didn't have those experiences yet.

When you are without a body, you are *pure love, unused and unaltered*. This love of yours can be altered and used in a lower-frequency realm, and there you can create new worlds. Without lowering the high frequency energy called "love" into a new, low-frequency energy called "fear," you wouldn't be able to live in and experience another part of God—the so-called evil part. You experienced and accumulated many experiences in lower dimension, both good and bad—whichever your soul decided—and that makes you God's heroes. Without those experiences lived on a lower-energy field, in the spirit world we would never know how you could live and survive in a negative energy.

We learned and had many experiences in a *conditional love* world. In the spiritual world, our concepts of living in denser energy fields have been informed and perfected, and now you have become God Masters. Many other species are watching you, looking for how you learned to lower your energy from *love* to *fear*. They are interested in learning how you raised the energy of *fear* to a higher-frequency level and then transmuted it into *love* and compassion. In other words, you are returning to the first form of love. Our understanding of the concept of fear is finally achieved. You are the pioneers who have opened and shown the way from darkness toward the light to civilizations from other universes. Now, they are more comfortable in taking a journey to a lower-frequency realm of conditional love.

When you come back home, we will honour you. We will have a big party for you to celebrate your completed mission, and every one of you will be named a master and a hero.

You have had experiences in this life (and in other lives) that have been positive and negative. The things that happened to you were caused by you only, because you are the creator of your own existence. Understand that, in the grand scheme of things, these experiences are important, and they are part of your contracts. Without them, we would never have accomplished what we had. You are heroes in God's eyes, performing roles with negative and positive energies. We signed a contract to complete these acts as either good or bad guys.

God's love *is all that is*, and now you are in the last phases of raising your frequencies of love necessary for your ascension. You belong to the source, who wants you back in the *love* energy field known to you as the source, or God, or the creator.

If you go back to the source, you have two options:

1. To stay with the source as light, or

2. Take a light body, and live as an immortal being on higher frequency levels called high dimensions.

I want to specify to you again that I am done with my role of lowering your vibrational energetic fields. I have done this by studying you and by altering your emotions and nervous systems. I found a way to manipulate you through your own bodily systems. Now you are at the final stage of your evolution in a lower-energy frequency, and you have created a dilemma for yourself. Which way should you take? Which road should you follow? You are still in doubt. Dilemma! Dilemma! It is time to decide.

Do you want to live in a lower-energetic frequency? Or, have you had enough of that frequency, and so you want to grow by going back to God's arms and living as *love?* It is your call. Your wish is God's command. I will respect and love you for whatever you choose. We, from the light, we honour you for your choices. We do not punish you, and we do not judge you for your decisions; instead, we love and respect you for your courage.

If you prefer the lower dimension, you will continue moving between human bodies, and will have similar experiences to those you've already had. If you choose to live in a light body, your future will be in a higher dimension called the "five dimension," which is a realm with a higher frequency.

Most of you are making mistakes, thinking of the dimensions as physical dimensions. I know your books teach you a little about dimensions, but the dimensions I am speaking about are linked to the frequency, vibration, and density of energy. The higher the frequency, the higher the dimension. You will not be conscious of the higher frequencies until you have experienced unconditional love.

In higher dimensions, we do not have the same needs as you. We have jobs that we love, and we live our lives in love, peace, joy, and bliss, and we interact and help each other. We do not need money or the structures you established in your lower dimension. Your lower dimension is only temporary, and when you live in such a low vibrational energy, you think it's very real and that's all there is. This sounds so real to you, because you live in fear, hate, and separation from yourselves and source.

When you and the Earth switch to a higher frequency, the game changes. Your third dimension is not that solid, so your DNA mutates, and your chakras vibrate at a higher frequency. At this point, your life becomes bliss, joy, and love. In a way, you change your body's structure from a carbon-based form to a crystal-line one.

Remember, you are made up of photons. A photon is known in your body as the energy released as light through the changes in energy metabolism. When your photons increase their frequency, you change as well. The higher your vibration/frequency, the higher the dimension you can reach. Understand that you are a part of God. It doesn't matter if you know that or not; it doesn't matter if you agree or not; and it doesn't matter if you believe it or not. Increasing your body frequency raises your consciousness, which is a state of awareness and understanding of one's own feelings, thoughts, existence, sensations, and emotions.

Now, before I go, I want to tell you a few things.

You read this book because I made you curious to learn more about me. You realize that we are all angels, no matter what your role is on planet Earth. We are helping each other to carry out the big divine plan. You realize that there is no hell or heaven, and you know that your real name is God. You understand that God—the source—is inside you. The name that you carry inside your body is called the soul, and it is a small part of God. You realize that we (you and me) are both the creators of your world through our thinking, words, actions, and reactions. You understand that I was your mentor and God for a short period, and that I led you toward destruction.

You also realize that your creation started with your own thoughts, and I had to alter that to achieve your soul's progression. You understand that I led you toward extinction, and that I had to change you slightly. I had to inhibit your DNA's function, and I only left two strands of DNA active; the rest had to be closed in order to successfully perform our plan. You realize that your thinking plays a significant role in your life's direction and that you attract what you focus on.

Dear ones, fear is an energy that I used to keep you controlled and enslaved and to shorten your lifespan. You realize that your belief system is changing with the constant programming of hate, black magic, and fear.

Think about this: if God gave you religions, why didn't He give you only one? Do you ever wonder why there are so many? This is because he gave you one, and then I used, multiplied, and changed religion according to my plan. How could I keep you in fear if you only followed one religion? I created many religions to keep you busy; you would argue with each other and create the energies of destruction and enslavement. You see, my partners in business, you can't flourish in this energy; you will end up destroyed. We have destroyed this world together a few times, and we have destroyed other planets too, in our distant past. If your religions were created by God, then—guaranteed—you would live in paradise and not in the hell I created for you, where you experience distress, poverty, hate, and war.

Understand that now is the time to break free from your chains and go home to the light. You are in that time where your karma is erased, and you are free to walk another level in your evolution: the level of love and light.

God delayed the process of ascension in order to give you more time to decide. He cannot do it forever, because it's not fair to the others who understood God's plan and the process of soul growth. You have to accept that you have to forgive and forget everything around you, including the people who have harmed you the most. Forgive them, and let them go. You will be much stronger after you do so. You will be so much lighter, and your health will improve.

You also have to change your programming and replace it with one that will serve you, rather than enslave you. Break free, my dear souls, for you are programmed in a way that makes me comfortable in controlling and oppressing you. Let go of the old programming, and go forward with a fresh one, which will open up your perceptions and receptions of divine codes. Your bodies are like computers, and they contain files that will make you frustrated and confused, and they will clutter up your mind. Delete the old files and install new ones. Don't override them, because they will not work. This will make you and your system tired, overburdened, and overwhelmed.

Break free, dear one. Break free from the chains we have created together. You have nothing to lose. Your new life will be brilliant, and it will have nothing that you have now: no wars, no fights, and no regrets. You will regain your power back—the power to create from a place of love, rather than fear and hate. Remember, you have nothing to lose. You will regain your love back, as well as your immortality, and you are not even aware of this. You are deeply loved and helped by me and other light beings from your galaxy, as well as those from other galaxies and universes. Do not fear us, for we are your family of light, and we love you unconditionally.

Remember what happens when you die. You leave the physical body, take a light body, and get on another level of existence. You take nothing with you—nothing of what you earned in your lifetime. You struggle, you work hard, and when you think that you have finished everything and you can relax, you leave the physical body and move on to another realm. It is a beautiful process, but it is also very hard for you to see the big picture the great divine plan. You are caught in the illusion of having just this lifetime. You are not aware that you are a light being who is wearing a physical body for a short period.

I love you dearly, and right now I am helping you with the light workers and light beings from the other universes and dimensions.

Together, we will restore you to your pristine condition, just like the one you were in before we started this project.

Be smart and choose *light* if you want to be happy, healthy, and live forever.

—*Lucifer*

Love Poems

I just wanted to let you know that I am a very romantic guy. And what is romanticism without a serenade? Because my scribe here doesn't know how to put my poems into musical notes, I decided that this would be a great opportunity to honour my loves from planet Earth with a few poems. In the beginning, my scribe didn't want to write them. After a few arguments, she agreed, and I am happy to tell you that I love you, and that I am holding you in my heart. As I told you before, I loved my women and wives with all my heart and soul. I dedicate the first poem to all the women of planet Earth, and to my wives, and the second poem is for my love from eternity, Ada. Most of you are on planet Earth now, and I hold you in my heart daily. You will recognize me if you look inside yourself, because you will find me there.

Enjoy!

—*Lucifer*

I Will Always Love You

I arrive at my destination,
and I want to send you my information,
that I loved you all the time,
and I looked for you on all lifelines.

You were my morning star,
shining day and night, and always far,
but my love for you never ceased,
and I looked for you from west to east.

I honour your love for me,
and I kept you always free,
because you were my precious treasure,
which, in gold, I couldn't measure.

You were my darling wives,
and you made me thrive,
because you all behaved innocently,
and I wasn't always with you decently.

I wasn't a perfect husband,
but I was a lovely legend,
and I treasure you more than diamonds—
more than all my funds.

I always carried you in my arms
with love, and a lot of charms.
I always fell in love with you,
and you never had a clue.

You never asked who I really was,
and you never bothered with my laws;
you loved me the only way you knew,
and our love was never askew.

My lovely princesses from my past,
our love always was a blast.
You amazed me with your grace
whenever I kissed your face.

I love you in eternity,
and I will serve you promptly,
because you were my entire world,
in my lovely dream world.

You are always on my mind,
and two hearts were aligned
in a pure love
when your heart I won.

I will cherish your love forever,
and would I leave you? Never!
You will never be far from my heart,
and we will never live apart.

Whatever you will do, sweetheart,
you will stay in my heart
as the most beautiful love story ever,
and would I forget you? Never!

I was an unhappy guy,
on your planet like a bad spy.
I always fell in love with you,
and you fell for me, too.

You didn't know who I was,
which made you more desired,
and I was looking through my glass technology
until I made myself tired.

You were my precious gift,
and with pleasure now, I give you a lift
toward other dimensions,
where there are other actions.

I will be with you all the way,
and I will protect you always
I will love you with all my heart,
and help you with all I've got.

You are my life, darling star,
and I created for you only war.
I hope you forgive me for all I have done,
now, in this last minute, before I run.

I will get you up in my arms,
and I raise you up with my charms.
I will kiss you all over,
because our time together is over.

I miss you when I'm under the moon,
and I can no longer be your groom.
I miss our time together,
but your time now is better.

I'll wait for your return home,
and your hair I will comb,
and we will fly together and reign
through constellations again.

And God will congratulate us—
you will get a mark of A-plus
for honouring your dedication to love
from the kingdom above.

Goodbye, and don't forget

that I have loved you since we met.
Goodbye, my queens of love
from the beautiful blue globe.

—Lucifer

Eternal Love

You are always on my mind,
and with me, you are gentle and kind.
I always treasure you,
and you were always new.

Running on your lifelines,
and taking a body that shines,
you marked my life forever,
and to all my dreams you answered.

You were all that I prayed,
and with my heart you played.
I hungered for your touch
when my heart you would catch.

You are my morning star,
coming each life on my radar.
I will never let you go
to eternity alone.

My lovely soul mate,
I will never regret
having you on all your timelines,
and helping you to shine.

I am your shadow from eons of time,
I followed you like a crazy guy,
I walked with you on all the lifelines,
and I raised you up into the sky.

I hold your love in my heart,
and you magically played your part.
I hold your magic in my dimension,
and I keep with me your affection.

Our love was one of a kind,
and I ran after you blind.
Our love was aligned
with all you designed.

You drove me crazy all the time
like no one can,
and I fell in love with you on each lifeline,
and I wasn't always your man.

Your love was like a thunder
burning in my heart;
you made my life blessed,
and our passion lasted until you departed.

Our love was full of magic,
and you never had a panic,
because I was different,
and our love was fervent.

When you took me in your arms,
and kissed me with your charms,
I would never forget your love,
because we fit together like a glove.

I cherish your love in eternity,

with passion and sensibility.
I wait for your return,
because my eternity you govern.

When you looked into my eyes,
I felt my love arise.
You surrounded my entire body,
and blessed me with a baby.

Our lives were magic,
and our love was cosmic.
I always carried you in my heart,
and you gracefully played your part.

I carry our love in eternity, stunned,
because you are my precious diamond.
We'll be together till the end of time,
and our love in the universe will shine.

—Lucifer